DANNII MINOGUE

My Style x

WITH PHOTOGRAPHS BY JONTY DAVIES

SIMON &
SCHUSTER
ILLUSTRATED

London · New York · Sydney · Toronto · New Delhi

A CBS COMPANY

First published in Great Britain in 2011 by Simon & Schuster UK Ltd
A CBS COMPANY

1 3 5 7 9 10 8 6 4 2

SIMON & SCHUSTER ILLUSTRATED BOOKS
Simon & Schuster UK Ltd
222 Gray's Inn Road
London
WC1X 8HB

WWW.SIMONANDSCHUSTER.CO.UK

Simon & Schuster Australia, Sydney

Simon & Schuster India, New Delhi

A CIP catalogue record for this book is available
from the British Library

ISBN: 978-0-85720-721-0

COMMERCIAL DIRECTOR:	Ami Richards
EDITORIAL DIRECTOR:	Francine Lawrence
ART DIRECTOR:	Nikki Dupin
PROJECT EDITOR:	Jane de Teliga
CONSULTANT EDITOR:	Charlotte James
PICTURE RESEARCHER:	Camilla Dowse
ADDITIONAL ARCHIVE PICTURE RESEARCH:	Nathan Smith
PHOTOGRAPHY:	Jonty Davies
HAIR AND MAKE-UP:	Christian Vermaak
STYLIST:	Angie Smith

DANNII MINOGUE WORLDWIDE MANAGEMENT:
Melissa Le Gear and Nathan Smith @ Profile Talent Management Pty Ltd

Printed and bound in Italy
Colour reproduction by Dot Gradations Ltd, UK

'Time Tested Beauty Tips' from *In One Era and Out the Other* reprinted by permission of
SLL/Sterling Lord Literistic, Inc. Copyright 1973 by Sam Levenson.

CONTENTS

FOREWORD BY KYLIE MINOGUE 4

Foreword
by KYLIE MINOGUE

Dannii and I experienced our first 'sister fashion moment' when Mum dressed us in matching outfits. Two items of clothing in the same section of the store and no bickering!

When we were little, shop-bought clothes were supplemented with home-made clothes – knitted jumpers, home-sewn corduroys, summer dresses, pyjamas. Mum made her share, but it was our grandmother, Millie, who whipped up all sorts of creations on her sewing machine right into our teens. The house was full of fabric and full of life. If it wasn't the whir of the sewing machine, it was the click-clack of knitting needles.

I think Millie, more than anyone, educated my sister and me about the mechanics of fashion. We learnt early on that you can create something nobody else has out of a remnant of fabric from the sale bin and a pattern. As we got older we became interested in what was 'fashionable' and realised that, with a little savvy styling, you can shape your own identity with the clothes you wear.

I, in turn, spent hours and hours at the sewing machine knocking up whatever my imagination concocted. It was love…

Around that time Dannii was in *Young Talent Time*, and was constantly immersed in a flurry of Lycra, sequins and all manner of showy get-ups. Her fashion radar had started to click ON!

I appeared as a guest on one episode of the show and, like all those years before, Dannii and I were dressed in matching outfits. But these ones took the biscuit… Silver sequined numbers and gravity-defying hair-dos (or should that be hair-don'ts?)!

It must have been a pivotal time for Dannii, not just in a sartorial sense but also in fostering her understanding of hair and make-up. There's no doubt she experienced more than your average teenager by spending hours in the wardrobe and make-up departments, and she had a lot of fun with it. I recall marvelling at her daring new hairstyles. She wasn't afraid to try the latest look.

I have a vivid memory of her coming home with a grey leather jacket on and all the family standing around her in awe… a leather jaaaaccckkeeeet!

I also know all the stuff she doesn't want you to know… like when she dressed up as Boy George to go to the Culture Club concert and shortly afterwards tried Prince's 'Purple Rain' look for a dress-up party. All very tragic, but tapping back into the tomboy style that started when she paired gumboots with a tutu at the age of about four. As a little tot it didn't matter what Danielle wore, she always looked cute like a little Kewpie doll (as does Ethan now).

Her style has come a long way since our childhood escapades fishing for tadpoles, helping Dad fix or wash the car, playing dress-up and making mud pies or whirly-whirlies in the pool before devouring huge slices of watermelon.

It's been joyful to watch Dannii's style evolve. My sister is now focused on deepening her knowledge of fashion and sharing what she has learnt. Her style has captivated her many admirers, and now they can take the next step on her style journey with her in the pages of this beautiful and personal book.

Kylie
xoxo

MY LOVE AFFAIR with FASHION

How I found my style

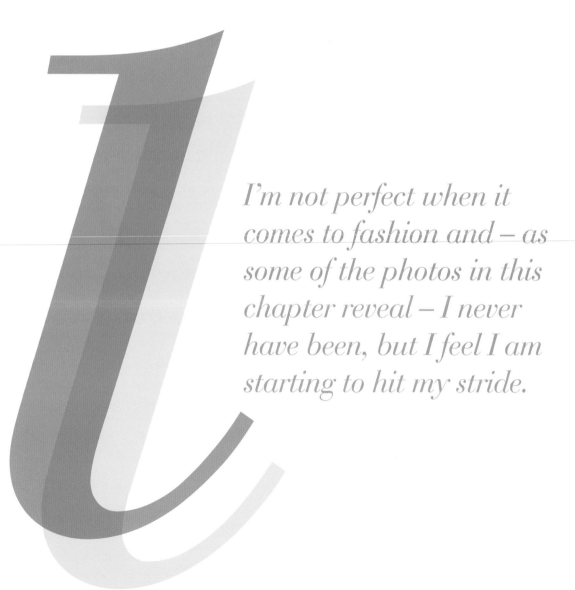

I'm not perfect when it comes to fashion and – as some of the photos in this chapter reveal – I never have been, but I feel I am starting to hit my stride.

{ *YOU ARE THE MASTER OF YOUR LOOK, AND NOTHING FEELS MORE FABULOUS THAN GETTING IT RIGHT.*

I adored turning 30, so much so that I had a badge with flashing lights that said: 'I am 30 years old today'. I looked forward to that birthday for two years, the way young girls look forward to turning 16.

It was a pivotal moment at which I started to feel comfortable in my own skin. I had made mistakes in fashion and life, and had gained enough experience to start putting it all together in a way that felt comfortable and relaxed to me. Really, getting older is just something to look forward to!

This book won't teach you how to look like me, or anyone else, but I hope it points you in the right direction and gives you some ideas on how to make the best of you. You are the master of your world and your look, and nothing feels more fabulous than getting it right.

PHOTOGRAPHED BY LEE BROOMFIELD FOR *INSTYLE UK*, AUGUST 2009

MY LOVE AFFAIR WITH FASHION: *MY STYLE*

MY EARLY STYLE

When I was three or four years old I used to wear yellow gumboots (aka Wellingtons), with the word 'stop' on the toe of the left boot and 'go' on the toe of the right boot. I'd team them with a tutu. My love of the eclectic was probably seeded in that outfit, which I wore quite happily anywhere my parents would let me. My style was born!

DANNII AND KYLIE

Kylie and I weren't big ones for dolls – we probably only had a couple of Barbies between us – but we did have a fabulous dressing-up box. Our grandma Millie helped us make all sorts of get-ups. As we got older, Kylie bought things at charity shops and flea markets. She is very good at that, and has the patience for trawling through things, chopping them up and reinventing them. I was always a fan of going to the fabric store and buying new, fresh, beautiful fabrics

SOME OF MY EARLY HAIRSTYLES AND (RIGHT) PLAYING DRESS-UPS WITH MY BROTHER, BRENDAN

and all the trimmings. Instead of having dolls we just dressed ourselves up, and that carried through to our adult lives. We've always loved going crazy with costumes for photo shoots and tours.

TINY TOTS

One of my very first jobs was as an extra on the Australian TV show *Young Talent Time* when I was about seven years old. I was in a group called the Tiny Tots, and when they needed kids to fill in the background of a scene, on we came. They provided the costumes but we had to bring our own little white canvas sneakers. I took the whitening of those sneakers very seriously, painting on the Kiwi shoe whitener myself to make sure they were whiter than white before I went off to work.

YOUNG TALENT TIME

The *Young Talent Time* wardrobe department was incredible. Barbara, the head of wardrobe, and her team of ladies worked their fingers to the bone because there were at least eight kids on the show at any one time, performing about

six new numbers a week. The number of costumes was huge but the budgets weren't, so there were rolls of fabric and rails and rails of stuff they'd made, put away, brought out again and reworked. It was like a giant dressing-up box.

As I graduated from the Tiny Tots to the Young Talent team, I started designing my own costumes for my solo numbers. From memory, I was the only member of the team who created their own costumes and I remember receiving fan mail from kids saying, 'Wow, where can I get that?' I used to write back explaining that it had been made at home with the help of my talented grandma. She showed me how to lay out a pattern on fabric and how to cut it out. I'd make suggestions about how I'd like to alter the patterns and she'd show me how to do that too. That's definitely where my love of design began.

Young Talent Time gave me an avenue to experiment with all the crazy stuff I'd
seen on music videos and in teen magazines — somewhere to express myself.
I was very into trends, and my influences came from music artists and popular
culture. Madonna was my main influence, with her crucifix, lace and net, little
gloves and the big teased hair.

GREASE

I loved the costumes in the film *Grease*. Sandy's big skirts and bobby socks were
mesmerising, and the moment when Olivia Newton-John transforms into sexy
Sandy wearing shiny black pants so tight they looked sprayed on and dances
with John Travolta, I was hooked. That was one of the pivotal fashion moments
of my childhood, and the scene bowls me over as much now as it did then.

ABBA

ABBA was another huge influence. They were so big in Australia — bigger than in any other market in the world — and their wild outfits totally captured my imagination. It's not that I would ever wear a gold Lurex bell-bottomed jumpsuit with white leather platform boots — I just thought their outrageousness was fabulous, and I admired and learned from the way they really owned their look, captivating music lovers across the globe.

WALKING IN HEELS

Young Talent Time was where I learned to walk, dance and do practically everything else in high heels. We had special dance heels designed for children's feet, so not like the crazy ones I wear now, but we'd be running around in them all day, so that's where I developed my arched, dancer's feet and my love of vertiginous, skyscraper heels.

AS TEENAGERS

When I was very little, I wore Kylie's hand-me-downs. I felt very grown-up wearing my big sister's clothes. When we hit our teenage years, things got more territorial. She had her style, I had mine, and there wasn't a lot of sharing going on! Because I was working I had my own pocket money, and could go out and buy whatever I wanted so we never fought over clothes. The Australian high-street chain Sportsgirl was a major fashion staple back then because they did bubble skirts like the ones Bananarama wore, which I loved. Now that we're 'big kids', the hand-me-down system has been reinstated. I'm slightly bigger in size than Kylie so, if she gets sent something that doesn't fit her and she thinks I'll love it, she'll send it over. I'm a big fan of that!

▲ A FASHIONABLE CHRISTMAS MORNING (TOP LEFT); HANGING OUT ON THE BEACH; A *TV WEEK* COVER FROM 1988; AND SINGING OUT ON STAGE

{ When we hit our TEENAGE years, Kylie had her style, I had mine, and there wasn't a lot of sharing going on! }

LIVIN' 80s STYLE

My stint on *YTT* coincided with the 1980s, possibly the most loathed era in fashion history. Much of the fashion was wrong – oh so wrong – but it was so much fun! The style of the era had real theatrical undertones: if you were going to do it then you did it completely OTT, big and bright and DayGlo and massive hair. It was a performance. Shoulder pads were the signature – a symbol of women's rising status in the corporate world and the hallmark of power dressing. Shoulder pads so broad we looked more like American football players than the beloved Melanie Griffith in the film *Working Girl*.

HOME AND AWAY

I worked with *Home and Away*'s producers, wardrobe and hair and make-up department to create the style for my character, Emma Jackson. Her leather jacket, heavy make-up and punky hair became quite iconic in the UK during this time. It was a signature 'bad girl' look.

WORKING WITH STYLISTS

My first real experience of working with stylists came when I started doing music videos. I worked with a girl called Alannah Hill, who started out as a stylist and is now an influential fashion designer in Australia. Back then, she was working in a boutique on Melbourne's Chapel Street. We got on really well and she helped with my styling for the *Love and Kisses* video with the leather jacket with the tattoo-printed sleeves and the giant gold crucifix, which I bought from Patricia Field's shop on my first trip to New York.

▲

MY COVETED
ENCRUSTED
BUSTIER (TOP
LEFT); ROCKING
THE INFAMOUS
LEATHER JACKET
AS EMMA JACKSON
IN *HOME AND AWAY*
(SECOND FROM
LEFT); AND
ASSORTED MUSIC
PROMO SHOTS
FROM THE 90s

WORKING IN JAPAN WAS ANOTHER EDUCATION IN STYLE.

▶

LONDON

When I first moved to London to promote my records, it was a whole new world with different labels and different trends. I was used to choosing what I wore but the stylists there were very specific, and I felt I had to listen to them because I didn't know the TV shows or the magazine covers I was going to be on. There wasn't time for me to get some London living under my belt and work out what styles and brands I liked, I just had to go with their advice and trust that they knew what did and didn't work for a UK audience. I found that quite difficult at times.

JAPAN

Working in Japan, where I also went to promote my records, was another education in style. The fashion scene there is all about crazy, different clothes and the stylists told me, 'You have to dress like this, otherwise it just doesn't work here and they won't print the pictures.' I was trying to find things I related to on the rails at shoots but I never really identified with the clothes. I felt like a fish out of water.

BIG 80s HAIR

The 1980s was the era of big hair and gallons of hairspray. I had long hair, so it took hours and hours to perm and I loved every minute of it. This was probably the biggest my hair got. My hairdresser had permed it and curled it with the hot tongs as well and wanted to get a photo of her curling work. I actually think perms are going to make a comeback in an updated way. Straighteners have ruled for so long, eventually something has got to change.

BLONDE HAIR

In the mid-1990s I decided I wanted to try life as a blonde. It definitely changes how you feel about yourself and the way people treat you! My hair grows very fast, so the re-growth was hell. I'd have to re-colour it every 10 days so I was a regular fixture at my hairdresser's. Great if you've got the time for it.

RED HAIR

In 1998 there was a hair disaster! I put a red colour through my hair to go

BIG HAIR
MOMENTS:
IN THE 1980s
(ABOVE) AND
MY BLONDE
INCARNATION
IN 1997
(RIGHT)

▲

AT A FANCY DRESS PARTY WITH ZANDRA RHODES
AND FRIENDS IN 1998; HAVING A 'WIG OUT' IN BLACK
AND BLONDE DURING MY 1991 CALENDAR SHOOT

as Farrah Fawcett to my 1970s-themed birthday party. The salon promised that it would wash straight out, but it was quite a bright red and guess what? It wouldn't budge. It was so permanent it was unreal! I stuck with it for six months, but I had to keep throwing more colour on it or it went a terrible faded red. Eventually I had to go back to brunette and wait until the red grew out.

WIGS

When I lived in London in the 90s I went through a phase where a friend and I used to wear wigs whenever we went out. I collected wigs that were very different from my real hair, which was, at the time, long and black. I had a short blonde one, a long fire-engine red one with a fringe and a short black one. I wore a wig for the photo of me posing as Elizabeth Taylor in *Cat on a Hot Tin Roof* and I wore an amazing curly red wig once from the BBC that had the nametag 'Joan Collins' inside it! Was it once Joan's, or did it belong to an actress playing her? I don't think I will ever know… I love the way wigs instantly change your look. Putting on a wig is the fastest, easiest way to take on a different persona. A wig or a wild outfit can give you the confidence to be the 'super you' and deliver the performance you're expected to give.

PHOTO SHOOTS TODAY

I've always been very happy to collaborate with top fashion stylists, and normally say to them: 'I have some ideas, but I'm not fixed on anything, and I'm excited to see what *your* vision is.' My job allows me to meet fabulous experienced stylists and gives me access to beautiful clothes from around the world. I've become friends with some over the years and have loved learning from them.

MY STYLE TODAY

I think things really started to come together just a few years ago. I knew who I liked and I knew what I liked. I had the option of working with stylists when I wanted to, but I could also go it alone – find a vintage piece and rework it or call up a PR company and get them to send me over a rail of dresses. It's taken ages, but now I'm finally comfortable with my style. I'm no longer second-guessing and wondering: 'Should I, shouldn't I, what will people think'? It's a good place to be.

These days, I'm more influenced by historical fashion than I am by trends. That's

GLAMOUR

www.glamour.com

MARCH 2010

ONLY £2 GLOSSY MAG WEEKLY PRICE!

OMG!
Dannii's
pregnant
*Where I'll
have the baby
*What Kylie
thinks!

50 SEX
QUESTIONS
you'd never
ask out loud –
answered

KISS YOUR
BODY HANG-UPS
GOODBYE!
Page 268 will crush
them for good

EXCLUSIVE INTERVIEW
David Cameron
wants GLAMOUR's vote?
Will he get it? Page 85

20% off
at Jaeger for
every reader

723+
STYLE FIXES
Splurges, steals – oh, and wait till
you see the SHOES! From £25!

ON SET IN MAY 2011 FOR THE *MY STYLE* SHOOT
AND (LEFT) WEARING ALEXANDER MCQUEEN ON
THE COVER OF *GLAMOUR* IN 2010

not to say I don't love watching catwalk shows but I tend to sit there spotting
the historical references. The designer I loved who was constantly cutting edge
and creating trends was Alexander McQueen. I was lucky enough to go to a
couple of his shows and they were always artistic spectacles. You never knew
what to expect. The runway could be covered with water, made of glass, or
in a disused warehouse. He always had something crazy going on. He was
constantly trying to make you re-evaluate fashion. I'll remember his shows my
entire life – he was a one-off. Lee, I salute you!

ELLE STYLE AWARD

This photograph was taken at the *Elle* Style Awards in 2005. The dress is by Céline and is a bias-cut column shift with embellishment at the neckline. It hung so beautifully, made me feel extra tall and the colour packed a punch. The French design house is right up my street, because they don't do anything too outrageous but their dresses always make a statement.

AN 'OMG' MOMENT

In March 2006 I was invited to the Céline fashion show in Paris. Paris Prêt-à-Porter shows are in a class of their own, because the city is so romantic and steeped in fashion history. I went over on the Eurostar; they put me up in a beautiful hotel and sent over a rail of beautiful clothes for me to choose from to wear to the show. For me, it was a special moment to be invited and sitting in the front row as the designer's guest. Afterwards, I went backstage and met Ivana Omazic, the Céline designer at the time. It was a gorgeous girly experience.

WITH KYLIE AT THE
ELLE STYLE AWARDS
IN 2005 (ABOVE)
AND AT THE PARIS
PRÊT-À-PORTER
SHOWS IN 2006
(RIGHT)

MY LOVE AFFAIR WITH FASHION: *MY STYLE*

'LOCK AND LOAD'

This picture was taken during Kylie's 'Homecoming' tour in 2006. Kylie's leopard print Dolce&Gabbana catsuit had matching ears and she told me the designers would make something to match for me. With or without the ears, I wondered? They made me the most divine tight black corseted bodysuit. It had a long piece of fabric at the back to cover my butt, but even so it took a fair bit of confidence to walk out on stage wearing it in an arena of 10,000 people. There was no way I was doing it without some serious reinforcements in the form of fabulous Capezio fishnets. They're proper dance ones that chorus girls wear, and they're so firm and stretchy they're like Spanx, sucking everything in. I wore two pairs, and each night I'd look up at my sister and say: 'Lock and load doll, lock and load!' I could run down the catwalk without the slightest jiggle. With the fishnets and the diamanté-encrusted microphones, we were living out every girl's pop-star dream.

ON SET AT THE *MY STYLE*
SHOOT 2011 (ABOVE) AND IN A
LEATHER CAP AND DOLLAR-SIGN
BLING IN 1991 (RIGHT)

HATS

I'm lucky that a lot of hats suit me, but my secret to that is wearing them on an angle. They don't suit me if I wear them pulled straight down on my head, but if I wear them at an angle they just seem to work, probably because it gives me more height. I believe there's a hat shape to suit everyone. It's just a question of finding it.

I'd love to wear more adventurous dressed-up hats. I haven't really got to that stage yet, but I think it's coming. The person who really knows how to rock a hat is Grace Jones. She has a firm friendship with milliner Philip Treacy, and has worn his hats for many years. I went to a retrospective of his work, where she strutted down the catwalk wearing an amazing hat, dragging a chair and belting out *La Vie en Rose*. It was breathtaking.

FINDING MY INNER LULU

I had a haircut in May 2009, and that was another major turning point for me. Looking back, it was the moment when my style became simple, chic and pared down.

My hair was breaking, so my Australian hair stylist, Fotini Hatzis, cut it off. What could have been a drama turned out to be a good thing. The new bobbed style she created was inspired by Louise Brooks – one of my style icons. Once I'd had the chop, I remember standing at the door to my wardrobe and realising none of my clothes went with my new hair-do any more – they belonged to the 'long-haired' Dannii.

It was exhilarating. I had a major closet clear-out and started to redefine my style in line with my new do. I bought myself the book: *Louise Brooks: Lulu Forever* (Peter Cowie, 2006) determined to immerse myself in her vibe, thinking: 'I've got to get my head around this.' From that point forward it helped me create my 'new look'.

THE NEW-LOOK BOB AT *COSMOPOLITAN* WOMAN OF THE YEAR AWARDS IN 2009 (ABOVE) AND MY STYLE ICON AND INSPIRATION, 20s SILVER SCREEN STAR LOUISE BROOKS (LEFT)

LOVE
my
STYLE
ICONS

Fashion icons who inspire me

I don't have any formal fashion training, but I have been lucky enough to work one-on-one with some of the best in 'the biz'.

I love collecting books on style and I study them avidly. Meeting people who have an amazing knowledge of fashion design and history has helped me to form my style.

FINDING YOUR STYLE

I believe the key to developing your own personal style is finding a timeless icon who has your body shape and looking at what works or worked for them in their heyday.

After all, they've had people working with them – couturiers or stylists – paid to help create 'looks'. They've already spent the money and done the hard work. All you need to do is adapt those styles and shapes and you're on to a winner – timeless style.

If you are a 'student of style', then you don't need any formal training – you can just pick things up as you go. Here are some of the icons whose looks I've drawn on over the years to evolve my own personal style.

Some of them weren't classically beautiful; they were just normal people with the same insecurities we all deal with. They didn't think they were the best things in the world, but they stopped men – and women – in their tracks and will live on as fashion and style icons forever.

WEARING A ROSE-TRIMMED MARCHESA DRESS; THE DANNII MANNEQUIN WEARS A J'ATON COUTURE CREATION

ICONS

A COUTURE
CREATION BY
CRISTÓBAL
BALENCIAGA
IN 1950

Design Icons

♡ CRISTÓBAL
BALENCIAGA

Amazing couturier Balenciaga
created fabulous, sculptural shapes
in the 1950s and 60s that much of
today's fashion is based upon. I can
look at a page in the book *Balenciaga
Paris* (Pamela Golbin & Fabien Baron,
Thames & Hudson Ltd, 2006) and
come up with a million design ideas
for my own fashion line, PROJECT D.
To me, he is just so inspiring.

Balenciaga Paris

◄ THE OH-SO-CHIC
ILLUSTRATIONS
OF RENÉ GRUAU

RENÉ GRUAU

One of the most famous illustrators in fashion history, René Gruau is an artist whose work I adore. I can spend hours, days even, looking at his illustrations. He was friends with Christian Dior, and created the House of Dior's bold, flowing look – sketching the famous illustrations used in their fashion plates and creating the looks for their fragrance campaigns. Gruau and Dior are inextricably linked through the history of fashion, and I love learning about their friendship.

ALBERTO VARGAS

Peruvian illustrator Alberto Vargas was famous for drawing 1940s pin-up girls and I've studied a lot of his pictures over the years. He's famous for his playful depiction of the sexy shape of women's bodies. While there's a lot of nudity in his sketches, his scantily clad women look so cute in the saucy clothing of the era. I'm really drawn to his illustrations because he only drew curvy women, and I feel I can relate to that.

▲
VARGAS AT
WORK IN
THE 1940s ON
HIS FAMOUS
PIN-UP GIRL
DRAWINGS

COCO CHANEL'S ICONIC STYLE FROM THE 30s STILL LOOKS MODERN TODAY

♡ COCO CHANEL

I have two words for people who say fashion is shallow or trite: Coco Chanel!
She is one of the greatest heroines in fashion history for making clothes
women could walk in. The godmother of relaxed dressing, she did away with
restrictive undergarments and figure-distorting dress shapes, and introduced
simple, elegant and – most importantly – functional styling.

In 1926 she shocked fashion circles (while simultaneously delighting women
the world over) by introducing women's trousers to her collection, and she
is credited as the inventor of the 'Little Black Dress' – the fashion staple
to end all fashion staples. Chanel changed the world! It's because of her
that women today feel comfortable in a sexy pair of trousers or look the
business in a tailored suit.

The Pioneer

♡ AMELIA EARHART

As the first woman to fly solo across the Atlantic, Earhart was doing a traditionally male job and wearing traditional male garments like one-piece jumpsuits. Today we don't even think about it when we slip on a pair of jeans, but back then a woman not wearing a skirt or dress was a major thing. You can't really imagine climbing into a plane with a skirt – whoosh! – but Amelia Earhart made it work. She made it elegant, and she's one of a handful of women who helped change fashion forever and helped carve out the way women dress today and how they defined themselves in the workplace.

AMELIA PIONEERED A NEW ANDROGYNOUS STYLE WEARING MASCULINE FLYING GEAR

♡ LOUISE BROOKS

The 1920s silver screen star Louise Brooks was the inspiration for my bobbed haircut in 2009. Owner of perhaps the sharpest bob in fashion history, Brooks is iconic; timeless. She wasn't the most classically beautiful woman, but I would describe her as handsome – and boy did she make an impact! Lulu taught me that finding your style is all about working with what you've got and bringing out the best in yourself.

♡ GRACE KELLY

I absolutely adore the 1950s American actress turned princess, Grace Kelly. She had a natural, elegant style and worked with amazing yet very simple shapes that are so timeless they look as good today as they did back then. I especially love the necklines she wore. Tabitha, my business partner, and I draw inspiration from her dresses for our PROJECT D label.

I was lucky enough to catch the Grace Kelly exhibition when it was on in Monaco. The collection included all of her dresses, the car that took her to Saint Nicholas Cathedral for her wedding in 1951 to Prince Rainier and her wedding gown, which was designed by Hollywood costumier Helen Rose. It was so delicate and elegant with its long sleeves, lace bodice and high collar, romantic, sheer veil, and she kept her hair and make-up very simple. I felt I caught glimpses of this in Catherine Middleton's wedding dress when she floated down the aisle of Westminster Abbey.

FROM MOVIE STAR TO PRINCESS:
GRACE KELLY'S STYLE STILL REIGNS

♡ AUDREY HEPBURN

Audrey Hepburn is another of my style icons. I'm not her shape – her physique was more streamlined than mine, so I can't emulate all of the things she wore – but I loved her style and beauty ethos. There is a poem by Sam Levenson, famously linked with Audrey Hepburn, which says, in a nutshell, that a woman's greatest asset is her attitude.

Style is not about the clothes you wear and how you wear them, it is about the person you are. We might be drawn to style icons because of a look, a piece of clothing or a haircut, but it's actually the essence of the woman that is alluring, captivating and which lives on. I will always remember Hepburn for the beautiful things she said, as much as for her physical beauty.

50s AUDREY
IN HER *ROMAN
HOLIDAY*-STYLE
CAPRI PANTS

TIME TESTED BEAUTY TIPS

For attractive lips,
speak words of kindness.

For lovely eyes,
seek out the good in people.

For a slim figure,
share your food with the hungry.

For beautiful hair,
let a child run his fingers through it once a day.

For poise,
walk with the knowledge you'll never walk alone...

People, even more than things,
have to be restored, renewed, revived,
reclaimed and redeemed and redeemed...

Never throw out anybody.
Remember, if you ever need a helping hand,
you'll find one at the end of your arm.

As you grow older you will discover that you have two hands.
One for helping yourself, the other for helping others.

SAM LEVENSON

THE POEM

Time Tested Beauty Tips

Contrary to popular belief, Audrey Hepburn didn't write this beautiful poem, it just happened to be one of her favourite poems and one she read to her sons. It was actually written by American TV host Sam Levenson for his grandchildren.

SOPHIA LOREN

Sophia Loren is one of my movie
icons because she's very, very curvy.
I've got a tiny waist like her, and love
to dress to emphasise that part of my
body. In her prime, Loren always wore
dresses that featured her waist, and
these images have become classics.
She's one of my ultimate style icons.

LAUREN BACALL

I love the way Lauren Bacall carried
herself, her understated sexuality
and the way she wore simple, clean
lines in classic colours. She was
almost as famous as Katharine
Hepburn for wearing pants and
the Bacall (slouch-style) trousers
are named after her.

♥ ELIZABETH TAYLOR

Elizabeth Taylor was another fabulous screen diva who knew how to rock her curves. If I search the internet for her name, lots of vintage pictures come up and I can see the gorgeous cinch-waisted dress shapes that worked on her and I know they will work on me. It's helped me find my style over the years.

ELIZABETH TAYLOR'S
FAMOUS ROLE IN
THE 1958 MOVIE
CLASSIC *CAT ON
A HOT TIN ROOF*

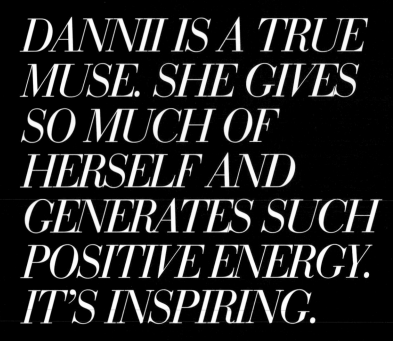

{ *DANNII IS A TRUE MUSE. SHE GIVES SO MUCH OF HERSELF AND GENERATES SUCH POSITIVE ENERGY. IT'S INSPIRING.*

J'Aton Couture

Modern-day Icons

♡ TWIGGY

A 'supermodel' before the term even existed, Twiggy embodies the 1960s. When I think of that era, she's one of the iconic faces that captures the mood, the time, the make-up and the clothes.

When she started out there hadn't been any models who were her shape or height or size – it was unheard of. Twiggy changed all that, and is a fabulous example of how to make the best of your shape.

BARBIE, BORN 1959, HAS A
BIGGER WARDROBE THAN
ANY GIRL IN THE WORLD

♡ BARBIE

You may not have expected her to
turn up on these pages alongside
Audrey Hepburn, Grace Kelly,
Elizabeth Taylor and Sophia Loren,
but Barbie is just awesome! Forget
Paris Hilton, forget The Queen, Barbie
has a bigger wardrobe than any girl
in the world is ever going to have…
ever! Best of all, it's jam-packed with
couture from the greatest designers
in history, all created specially for her.
Barbie's little pink heels are iconic in
their own right.

KATE MOSS

A modern-day style icon, Kate has compiled an incredible fashion portfolio in front of the camera working with the best in the business. If you combine that with the way she dresses day-to-day when she's running around on her own time, she is evolving into a timeless fashion icon. When you see paparazzi pictures of Kate you know her look: a mixture of vintage and expensive pieces to create a signature style that always looks effortless.

▲

MODERN-DAY ICON KATE MOSS MIXES DESIGNER, HIGH STREET AND VINTAGE FOR HER COOL ROCK CHICK STYLE

VICTORIA BECKHAM

I love that Victoria's personal style has evolved – she's discovered it along the way. She didn't go to fashion school, but she has learnt from people she has worked with and studied fashion.

She puts a tremendous amount of work into her designs. The inside structure of her dresses is as incredible as the outside, and there are very few designers you can say that about. Victoria's dresses have a structure that you don't see, but it makes you walk a different way and alters your posture. Her designs are works of art. I really admire the fact that she hasn't left anything out. She's gone the whole nine yards to make her designs the best of the best of the best.

▶

VICTORIA
BECKHAM
WEARS
HER OWN
SLEEK
DESIGNS
IN 2009
(RIGHT)
AND 2010
(FAR RIGHT)

LOVE MY STYLE ICONS: *MY STYLE*

WEARING A
VICTORIA
BECKHAM DRESS,
PHOTOGRAPHED
BY JONTY DAVIES
FOR THE COVER OF
MARIE CLAIRE UK.
JANUARY 2011

57

MY FAVOURITE FASHION BOOKS

I love collecting books on fashion. If anyone ever asks me what I would like as a gift, the answer is always a beautiful book on style.

Some of the books that are the pride of my collection:

- *Manolo Blahnik* by Colin McDowell
- *Resort Fashion* by Caroline Rennolds Milbank
- *The Art Of Barbie* by Craig Yoe
- *Fashion Illustrator* by Bethan Morris
- *100 Years Of Fashion Illustration* by Cally Blackman
- *Dior* by Alexandra Palmer
- *Fifty Dresses That Changed The World* by The Design Museum
- *The Goddess Guide* by Gisèle Scanlon
- *This Little Piggy Went To Prada* by Amy Allen
- *People In Vogue: A Century Of Portrait Photography* by Robin Derrick and Robin Muir
- *Bernard Of Hollywood...* by Bruno Bernard
- *Balenciaga Paris* by Pamela Golbin and Fabien Baron
- *Alberto Vargas* by Alberto Vargas and Reid Austin
- *Vintage Fashion* by Emma Baxter-Wright
- *Put On Your Pearls Girls* by Lulu Guinness
- *Grace Kelly, Princesse du Cinema* by Stanislas Choko
- *Louise Brooks: Lulu Forever* by Peter Cowie

I Love
DRESSING UP

Red carpet and all that jazz

I love classic, elegant, old school Hollywood glamour when it comes to red carpet dressing.

The look is gorgeous, healthy and natural. Nothing too OTT or overdone – it's about getting it just right. As I am only 5'2" I look for well-fitting dresses that elongate my body, shoes that look beautiful on my feet and go with the dress, and a small, elegant clutch.

DRESS BY MARTIN GRANT, PARIS; DIAMOND JEWELS BY JOAAL

I LOVE DRESSING UP: *MY STYLE*

MY *Top 10* RED CARPET LOOKS

PHOTOGRAPH BY JONTY DAVIES FOR *MARIE CLAIRE UK* IN 2011

I LOVE DRESSING UP: *MY STYLE*

1 BUSTLING ABOUT

My all-time favourite, I wore what I now call my 'Bumblebee' dress to the National Television Awards in London in 2010, just after the news of my pregnancy broke.

It was designed by Victor Costa, who's been known as the 'King of the Copycats' since the 1950s for his skill at translating the catwalk designs of couturiers like Christian Lacroix into affordable New York fashion.

Made from cream silk and black velvet, Bumblebee has definite Lacroix overtones, with its big bustle and the black netting that peeks out from underneath the skirt at the back.

I found it at a vintage shop in London called Atelier Mayer, and my favourite Melbourne design duo, J'Aton Couture, altered it to fit me. My dad, who's not a 'fashion junkie', said that even though the dress was vintage and had its own history, it looked as if it had been made for me.

There was extra attention on me that night because a lot of people were looking for the baby bump, but this dress gave me extra confidence. I felt my little baby was wrapped up and protected in my prom-style dress.

'I found Bumblebee
in a vintage shop
in London called
Atelier Mayer'

WITH KYLIE
AT THE
ELLE STYLE
AWARDS, 2010

2 ILLUSIONS OF SLENDER

This photo was taken at the *Elle* Style Awards in 2010 when I was four months pregnant. It didn't matter what I tried on that day, all you could see was the bump. Then I popped on this dress by Sydney-based designer Lisa Ho and suddenly it was: 'Where did it go?'

With vertical pleats running the length of the dress, soft draping and a split in the skirt, this dress is typical Lisa Ho – pretty and easy to wear – and the asymmetric neckline really stretched me out. If you want to look taller, the more vertical lines you have the better.

Kylie presented me with the Best TV Star award that night, so this photo holds very special memories for me.

3 OUTTA SPACE

This J'Aton creation was for the 2009 MTV Awards in Sydney. I'm always scared to do something new on the red carpet and I rarely wear anything above the knee, so this dress felt incredibly risqué for me. The boys at J'Aton wanted to do something very different, and because it was couture and they'd made it to fit me, I trusted them. It was corseted all the way down the back with a peplum-like band at the hipline. Very space-age.

4 STATUESQUE

I worked from scratch with J'Aton Couture to create this Grecian-style dress for Australia's Logie Awards in May 2009. Cutouts are not usually my thing, but with the draping from the shoulder and the little slice of skin, it is reminiscent of a sari, making it incredibly feminine. We tried to capture the shapes and textures of a Grecian marble statue in the hemline of the dress, using chunky, futuristic-looking elastic to create heavy, textured folds. A Grecian, Indian, futuristic dress with a 1920s Louise Brooks bob and Egyptian make-up... Perhaps it shouldn't have worked but I loved it!

IN TWO OF MY FAVOURITE RED CARPET DRESSES BY J'ATON COUTURE, 2009

5 LADY LUCK

I needed a dress for our PROJECT D launch at Selfridges in May 2010 and our samples were stuck in transit because of a freak-of-nature volcanic ash cloud. This dress, 'Casino', was the only one we had in my size, and it's lucky it was stretchy or I'd have had nothing to wear that night. You'd never think the elements of this look would work. Big tummy? I know, I'll cover it in stretchy skin-tight sequined fabric!! Even though it was not a maternity dress, I still get comments from women saying it's the best maternity evening dress they've ever seen!

6 RED CARPET ARIA

We christened this dress, which I wore to *Cosmopolitan*'s Fun Fearless Female Awards in November 2009, my Sydney Opera House dress. It was drawn in like a pencil skirt on one side, and the other side was constructed out of three wired rolls like the sails of the Opera House. The fabric is distressed silk, so when you look from a distance the dress looks crisp, but close up it has a soft fragility to it. It is one of J'Aton's wilder creations, and I used to see it on a mannequin when I visited their atelier. Nobody else 'gets it', they said, but for me it was love at first sight. I would have it made in every colour of the rainbow if I could.

'I must have been feeling gutsy that night to wear this emerald green dress on the red carpet'

7 LA DOLCE VITA

I wore this dress by Dolce&Gabbana to the Australian Film Institute Awards in 2006. It's a classic shape that, with a bit of contemporary styling, would still work tomorrow or in 10 years' time. The heavily corseted bodice is typical of the label's sexy, lingerie-inspired design. Looking back, I must have been feeling gutsy that night to wear this emerald green colour down the red carpet. I did my best to channel their famous *Dolce Vita* vibe.

WEARING EMILIA WICKSTEAD (LEFT) AND (BELOW LEFT)
MY FIRST VICTORIA BECKHAM DRESS IN 2009

8 VIVA ITALIA

I wore this red two-piece to the press launch for
The X Factor final last year. The designer, New Zealander
Emilia Wickstead, specialises in made-to-measure
wear, and this little number is fitted within millimetres
everywhere, doesn't budge an inch and feels phenomenal.
Wickstead spent her teenage years in Italy, and this outfit
is a real nod to an adolescence spent steeped in Italian
fashion. I can imagine wearing the little top on its own
with black Capri pants and little ballet flats, hopping
on the back of a Vespa, riding through the streets of
Rome, then whipping the skirt on over the top when I
arrive at my party! Think Audrey Hepburn in the movie
Roman Holiday.

9 CURVY CLASSIC

Women's curves never go out of fashion, and
this Victoria Beckham dress enhances the
classic 1950s hourglass silhouette perfectly.
This was the first time I'd worn one of Victoria's dresses,
and the inner structure is incredible. It has a belt at the
waist, a corset, then the outer dress zips up over the top.
So even though it's strapless, it holds itself up and there's
no way it's going to move. It felt fabulous.

I LOVE DRESSING UP: *MY STYLE*

WITH ANTHONY
AND JACOB
FROM J'ATON
IN 2009

10 GETTING SHORTY

I don't know how the J'Aton boys got me into a dress so short for the 2009 Melbourne Fashion Festival, but they must have caught me at an odd moment when I was quite happy to show my legs. I love the layering of this dress. The under-bodice is nude with the sort of gold piping detail that you'd normally see on corsetry, and the overdress is lace, which softens the hemline and, I always think, makes the legs look more elegant.

WHAT TO WEAR?

Dress to suit the occasion

If you've ever found yourself cross-eyed trying to figure out the dress code on an invitation, you're not alone. Many a disappointed party-goer has been tripped up by their designer trainers or caught short in a thigh-skimming mini when a ball gown was actually the go.

Here's a foolproof dress code decoder that I follow so I'm never caught out 'couture challenged'.

TEST RUNNING A CHIC NUMBER BY ROLAND MOURET

I LOVE DRESSING UP: *MY STYLE*

- **CASUAL:** Anything goes! Jeans, shorts, combats, kaftans or Capri pants… Exercise your personal style with confidence.

- **SMART/CASUAL:** Perhaps the most ambiguous of the dress codes, what qualifies as smart/casual at one venue will see you stranded in the street outside another. Generally if you're nicely presented – ladies in a dress or trousers with appropriate accessories, men wearing a tailored (sports) jacket and pants and a light-coloured shirt – you can't go wrong, right? Actually no! A tie or even a suit may or may not be required and some places will turn away designer denim and diamond-encrusted trainers! The top tip is to call ahead to the venue or party host to make sure you get it just right.

- **GARDEN PARTY:** Ladies, here's your chance to wear a pretty, flowing dress – avoiding long hemlines that drag on the ground. Men should stick to smart/casual, perhaps opting for a light-coloured suit in hot weather.

- **INFORMAL:** Don't be fooled, this does not mean casual! Men, wear a dark suit; ladies, wear a short (anything but evening-length) dress.

- **LOUNGE SUIT:** Lots of options for the ladies here – a pretty dress, smart suit or a cocktail dress (for an early evening event) will all pass muster. For the men, it's a dark suit, white shirt and nice tie.

- **COCKTAIL** (After 5pm): Now we're really starting to stretch our sartorial legs! Glamorous frocks and fabulous accessories for the ladies, a suit (ideally dark) and tie for the men.

- **BLACK TIE OPTIONAL:** This dress code clues you in that formal attire is required. Men have the option of wearing a dinner jacket or a dark suit and tie; women should wear a cocktail or long evening dress.

GET READY FOR YOUR CINDERELLA MOMENT . . . GLASS SLIPPERS OPTIONAL

HOLDING A GOLD
BROCADE STUNNER
FROM MARTIN GRANT

- **BLACK TIE** (After 4.30pm):
Out come the lush evening dresses
for the ladies while the men get to
channel their inner James Bond
in a dinner jacket, matching black
dress pants and – my favourite –
a black bow tie.

- **WHITE TIE** (After 6pm):
Ready for your Cinderella moment?
White tie is super-formal, with men
in black tailcoat, black trousers,
white waistcoat and a self-tied bow
tie and ladies in evening dresses.
Glass slippers optional!

How to find the dress

Receiving the odd last-minute invitation can put us all in a spin, looking in the wardrobe and throwing our hands in the air saying, 'I have nothing to wear.' Well, not the perfect dress anyway.

Here are some tips for finding that 'million-dollar' dress:

There's nothing better than buying off the peg and having a garment tweaked to fit you – I do it all the time and it gives clothes that made-to-measure feel, making them look sharper and more expensive.

Know what suits you and shop with a shape in mind. Find a picture of the style of dress you're looking for and take it with you. This is where your icons – those with a similar body shape and style to yours – come into their own. Use your favourite pictures of them to keep your search on trend and on track.

Once you find a dress that you love, don't be scared to buy it in other patterns or colourways. This can solve any last-minute couture crises.

Reduce your chances of bumping into someone else wearing 'your' dress at a party by buying a pattern, then either make it yourself or have it made. If you're adventurous, eliminate the chance of 'fashion clashin'' by making minor adjustments that ensure your frock is unique.

You can't beat an experienced eye, so if you find someone local who's really good, ask them how to alter something so it will fit you better. Get them to explain what they're doing so you learn how to tweak your clothes to perfection every time.

Think you've already got the right dress in your wardrobe? You can't improve on perfection, so why try? Take your dress to a local tailor or seamstress and get them to copy it in another colour or fabric.

Why you should befriend your local tailor or seamstress

When you're buying off the peg, and depending on your individual body shape, you'll find there are always things that don't quite fit right. I'm vertically challenged, petite and short in the waist, so most of my clothes have to be taken in and up, and the sleeves narrowed.

What would I do without Dorothy? Dorothy is a seamstress at a local shop in London who was recommended by a friend. I don't know how I survived without her. She has worked on everything from hemming jeans to intricate couture pieces, made things for me from scratch, and copied an item already in my wardrobe. There is nothing she can't do!

I find myself saying, 'You're not going to like me this week. I have a dress that I'm not sure we can make work and I need it in two days' time'. Dorothy's answer is always the same: 'I love a challenge!'

The couture process

There are no hard and fast rules when you're creating couture – it depends on the couturier you're working with.

Tamara Ralph of Ralph & Russo draws and draws when she feels creative, and I flick through her sketchbooks to find something I love or that I want to adapt. With J'Aton, I'll go to their atelier for one dress, and we'll come up with 10 ideas and perhaps make eight of them. Many of their customers are brides-to-be; they have fun designing things that are a little bit different for me.

A couturier will ask you what the event is that you're dressing for, whether you have to travel to get there, will you be sitting down or standing all night or dancing? And they'll ask you whether you want it short, long, asymmetrical, conservative or outrageous. If you have an idea of what you're looking for, they'll ask you what you like about it. Is it the colour, shape, the retro style, that it's bold or looks like lingerie? They'll chip in some ideas that maybe you haven't thought of before. With couture, it's all about narrowing things down. You start with all the possibilities and keep saying no until you are left with just the elements that make the dress perfect.

Next come the fittings. The couturier will probably take your measurements on the spot, and they'll want to know how far away the event is and the likelihood you'll be the same size and shape when party time rolls around.

Most designers will fit you with a toile – a dress base made out of calico or another cheap fabric that they'll pin on to you, drawing in darts and seams so that the measurements are perfect. They will work from this toile until they are ready to cut the fabric for your dress.

{ I love seeing ROLLS OF FABRIC
— the possibilities are endless. }

At the next fitting, you'll try on the dress in the real fabric so you can see how it folds and falls. This is the point at which you need to speak up if you want to make any radical changes. You should take shoes of the right height with you to this fitting, even if they're not the final shoes. If the designer will let you, it's great to take a photo of the dress at this stage so you can go and find shoes, accessories and start thinking about hair and make-up.

ANGIE
LOVES

The style consultant

During the 2010 series of *The X Factor* I was pregnant, juggling about five different projects and simply didn't have time to do all my own styling, so I teamed up with style consultant Angie Smith.

I knew I wanted to use some familiar designers, but also inject some fresh talent into my wardrobe. I brought a mood board to my first meeting with Angie. There were many images – but one in particular summed up the way I wanted the whole series to feel – and there were pictures of the shapes and styles I love, with the all-important colour palette. I tried on all the dresses I'd brought back from Australia, we photographed them and she sourced jewellery, accessory and shoe options. Sometimes she'd introduce me to a new designer, sometimes she'd track down something I'd seen in a magazine or on the catwalk. Occasionally she'd arrive at the show with a huge tray of jewels and tell me to take my pick. When she couldn't make it along to the studio, she'd send all the options and I'd style it up myself. I love the collaboration – it is great to have someone to bounce ideas off.

My TIPS and TRICKS for looking great for that special event...

● **PICK A COLOUR THAT SUITS YOUR SKIN TONE.** It might be tempting to experiment with this season's hot shades, but that should start and end in the shop fitting room.

● **KEEP IT SIMPLE.** Make sure the different elements of your ensemble don't clash with one another. If you have too much going on, people won't be looking at your face.

● **KEEP YOUR HAIR AND MAKE-UP LIGHT AND NATURAL LOOKING.** If the event is special, chances are there will be photos, and you don't want to look back and wonder why you painted your face like a Bratz doll.

● **ONCE YOU'RE DRESSED WITH HAIR, MAKE-UP, ACCESSORIES, BAG AND SHOES,** do a 360-degree twirl in front of the mirror.

● **WALK AWAY, COME BACK AND DO IT AGAIN.** Does something jump out at you? Whatever it is, I suggest you take it off, because if you're noticing it, it's probably too much!

● **GET SOMEONE TO TAKE A DIGITAL PHOTO OF YOU, FRONT AND BACK.** Is there anything showing that shouldn't be, anything not quite right about your outfit? A photo is the best way to play fashion detective because it reveals what others see.

The stylist

I work with stylists on magazine cover shoots. The
editor and creative director will have an idea in mind,
and a mood board of photo references to help everyone
understand what they're aiming for. After this, the stylist
pulls pieces from designers that will look good on me.
We'll go through a rail of clothes, narrowing down the
options. Then we'll show the photographer, who might
veto some pieces. In the end we'll probably shoot two or
three different outfits so the editor has options for the
cover. I'm like an actor creating a character, and often
end up wearing something I'd never normally wear.
Hair and make-up artists help bring the fantasy to life.

I worked with stylist Jayne Pickering for the *Marie Claire*
January 2011 cover shoot. She'd studied what I wear,
knew the styles I love and those she thought really suited
me. It was a 'moment'. She picked out the exact dresses I
would have chosen for myself – if only I had the time, a
team of style elves and the direct lines for these wonderful
designers. There was one dress, a Valentino ball gown
with a huge skirt, that caught my eye. I didn't care if the
photographer didn't want to shoot it; I had to at least try it on.
The theme of the shoot was paparazzi, and the photographer
thought it would be amazing to photograph me on the
cream leather seats of a Bentley, and I was imagining it with
me wearing this amazing ocean of dress. The photographer
and stylist really felt it would work, and this was the result.

PHOTOGRAPH BY JONTY DAVIES FOR *MARIE CLAIRE UK* IN 2011

THE FOUNDATION

My underwear secrets

With all the brilliant products around these days, for me there's no excuse for nipples or knicker lines to be on display when you're in your party finery. Good underwear is the solid foundation on which style is built. The people who do red carpet well might have the personal trainer and the special-event diets, but they also have all the tricks going on underneath the dress.

DRESS BY MARCHESA WITH EARRINGS BY ANNOUSHKA

THE PERFECT BRA

A bra that fits perfectly can completely transform your décolletage and make you feel – and look – like a new woman. In London, Rigby & Peller is famous for its bra fitting, sizing and alteration services. The size of a woman's breasts fluctuates constantly. To avoid the horrors of four boobs and back cleavage, Rigby & Peller recommends we have our measurements checked every six months. Most department stores and lingerie shops have in-house bra fitters these days. You may discover you're a different size in different brands – you'll most certainly discover that you feel good and look great when you're wearing the right foundations. You don't need to buy dozens of different bras, you just need a couple that fit really well. It all comes back to making the most of your assets. One brand I love is Aussie label, Pleasure State.

SEAM-FREE KNICKERS

Seam-free knickers are the only way to guarantee you will avoid VPL. In London, Marks & Spencer sells seam-free 'no VPL' knickers in every possible style, from boy shorts through to thongs. The trick is to always wear nude colour underwear under white because if the fabric of your clothing is at all see-through, white under white will show through.

SPANX

Possibly the greatest fashion invention of the 21st century (and the company was only established in 2000 so that's not bad going), Spanx is a range of body-shaping underwear that smooths and streamlines the figure, helping you to retain a fabulous shape in the face of close-fitting cuts and clingy fabrics.

Why I will never be French!

Englishwoman to Parisian woman: 'Is it true that you never leave the house without matching underwear?' Parisian woman to Englishwoman: 'There is another way??'

I'm constantly building up a foundation underneath the dress I'm wearing. If the dress has a low neckline, I'll wear a plunge bra that doesn't match my anti-VPL, seam-free big knickers. Sometimes it's a Spanx half slip that is stretchy, holds everything in and smooths me out but most definitely doesn't go with my bra. Oh la la. . . That's why they'll never give me a French passport!

HOLLYWOOD FASHION TAPE

A genius Aussie range of red-carpet-ready products including 'CoverUps' and 'No-Shows' – respectively reusable and disposable nipple concealers that ensure you leave a little something to the imagination – are essential when you're going bra-free.

HOSIERY

The right hosiery can put the perfect finishing touches to an outfit, and deftly update an ensemble from day to evening wear. I love opaques and boots for winter, and there's nothing like a pair of sheer stockings with seams down the back for a touch of sexy sophistication. Then there are the lock and load Capezio fishnets of Kylie's Homecoming Tour fame. They look fab and they're the pantyhose equivalent of Spanxs. Love it!

CLOSE ENCOUNTERS
OF THE FABULOUS KIND

VALENTINO

My friend Benjamin Hart – a former model and fashion expert – brought Valentino Garavani along to *The X Factor* in 2010. I was wearing one of our own PROJECT D designs called 'Tinsel' from our Holiday Collection that night.

Imagine my reaction when Valentino, an icon of 20th-century fashion and a man who's created some of the most beautiful gowns in fashion history, said words to the effect: 'Wow, you look great in this dress, what is it?'

What do you do in that situation? We're talking about the man who created Julia Roberts' show-stopping vintage black-and-white gown that she wore when she accepted her Oscar in 2000. Do you just say a simple thank you??

Well, after closing my gaping jaw, I threw caution to the wind and said: 'Thank you, this is my design, so you've made my life!!'

If all this stopped tomorrow, I'd be a happy woman after that particular fashion moment.

READING THE VALENTINO RETROSPECTIVE BOOK IN TUCKER TOP

DOLCE&GABBANA

Fabulous Italian design team Domenico Dolce and Stefano Gabbana are world famous for their sleek, sexy designs. I was touched by this humble email from them after I wore their beautiful creations on *The X Factor* results shows in 2010.

Dearest Dannii,

This is a quick note to say how beautiful you looked on *The X Factor* recently wearing not only the floral print dress but also the black fitted dress! Let us take this opportunity to thank you for your continued support of the Dolce&Gabbana brand!

Love from Italy,

DOMENICO & STEFANO

This note says so much about every stitch that goes into every garment they create. There is a saying, 'Some people cook with love.' Dolce&Gabbana design with love.

LOVE IT

Dannii Minogue looked so beautiful in #victoriabeckham last night!!!!!!!!!!!X vb X

17 Oct via Twitter for BlackBerry®   ☆ Favorite ↄ⊃ Retweet ↩ Reply

VICTORIA BECKHAM

I loved Victoria's little tweet after I wore the stunning Champagne-coloured column dress from her Autumn/Winter 2010 collection on *The X Factor*. I'm a huge fan of Victoria's creations. I'm so impressed by her commitment to her label and her attention to detail in every part of her fashion empire. I wore her fabulous sapphire-coloured drape dress from the same collection on the following Sunday night's results show.

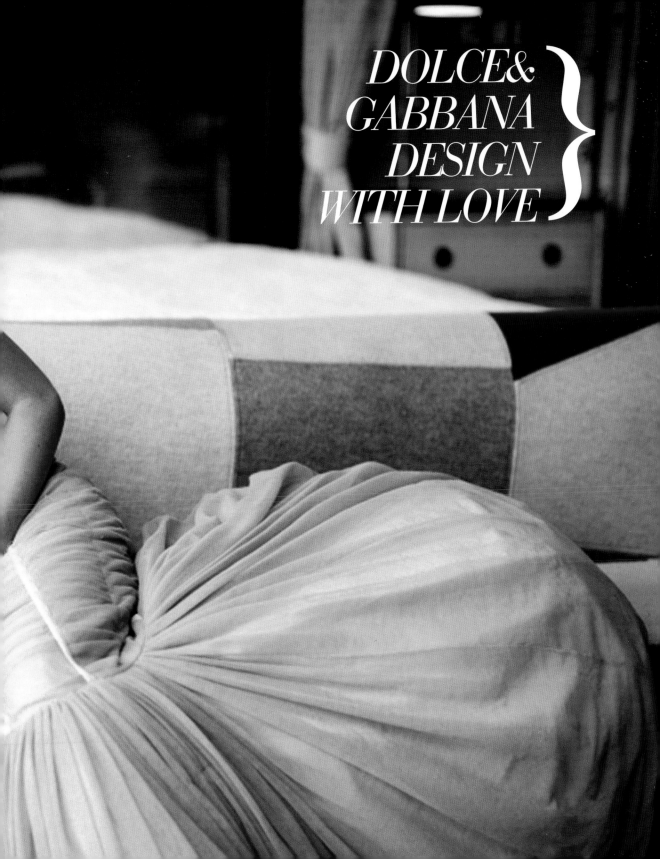

DOLCE&
GABBANA
DESIGN
WITH LOVE }

SOME OF MY FAVOURITE DESIGNERS

J'ATON COUTURE

The Australian design duo J'Aton Couture is my favourite couture designer team. Jacob Luppino and Anthony Pittorino created several of the dresses I wore on *The X Factor* in 2010. Like me, they're sticklers for detail, and their bold, unique designs pack a punch on stage or on the red carpet.

ELIE SAAB

I love the way Elie Saab infuses classic red-carpet glamour with unique touches. When women slip on an Elie Saab gown they seem to truly find their style. He's not outrageous, just modern and edgy, making him a favourite of A-listers like Beyoncé. He definitely has a 'wow' factor!

BEJEWELLED DRESS BY J'ATON COUTURE

96

MARCHESA

English duo Georgina Chapman and business partner Keren Craig own the red carpet with their elegant, old-Hollywood designs. A former actress, Georgina has the poise of a ballerina and that sensibility is reflected in her designs. She seems to possess a unique understanding of the body, how to hang things off it, and how the cut of a dress can change a woman's posture. Their New York-based label is a red-carpet favourite of a whole host of stars, including Sandra Bullock, Demi Moore and Sarah Jessica Parker.

EMILIA WICKSTEAD

While born in New Zealand, Emilia spent her formative years in Milan with her fashion designer mother Angela, living and breathing Italian fashion. She shows ready-to-wear designs in her Pont Street boutique in London, but she will make them to measure, so it's almost couture at ready-to-wear prices. She's all about simple shapes and 1950s elegance, the style she's been immersed in since her childhood. Her designs are feminine, understated, luxurious and timeless.

RALPH & RUSSO

The London-based Aussie design team of Tamara Ralph and Michael Russo is a long-time favourite of mine. Their glorious gowns start as hand-drawn sketches and are handmade to measure, each one taking days (or even weeks) of stitching, beading and embellishing to complete. Now, that's what I call attention to detail!

RALPH & RUSSO GOWN, JASPER CONRAN FEATHER BOLERO, AND DECO EARRINGS AND DIAMOND BRACELET BY BENTLEY & SKINNER

I LOVE DRESSING UP: *MY STYLE*

Tips for wedding day dressing

The boys from J'Aton say: 'A girl's wedding is the most important red-carpet event of her life. At least at the Oscars there are other, equally high-profile attendees, but on your wedding day all eyes are on you.'

Here are their tips for wedding day dressing:

Don't just look at bridal wear when choosing a gown. Most brides only look at wedding dresses, which can mean their personality and individuality is lost in the dress. Consider adapting something you've seen on the red carpet for a unique look.

Queen Victoria set the precedent for white bridal wear. Royal brides before her typically opted for heavy silver brocade. Red was a particularly popular colour in Western Europe and in the 1800s black wedding dresses were popular in Finland, so why does 21st-century bridal dressing come with such a conservative rulebook?

A ROSE-TRIMMED, WEDDING-PERFECT HAT BY PHILIP TREACY

> The KEY to getting wedding dressing right is to feel completely represented and confident in your choice of gown. You must own and possess the gown in all its glory or simplicity. You must wear the gown and not have the gown wear you.
>
> *J'Aton Couture*

When you're on the hunt for the perfect wedding dress, start the search in your own wardrobe; take a look at the cuts and styles that have always suited you. If a particular neckline suits you for everyday dressing, it will suit you in your bridal gown. The trick is to make it just that little bit more luxurious and special.

Dress for you, then dress for your partner. You enter marriage as two becoming one, so it's your time to shine for you and your intended. Don't dress for your best friend or your mum. Be inspired by them, perhaps, but ultimately this is about the nuptials.

Consider making your gown extra meaningful by taking a piece of Mum's wedding gown or headdress, some of the beads, a section of lace, and having it hand sewn on to your own gown to create a piece of history and a future heirloom to pass on to loved ones.

ELIZABETH TAYLOR
ARRIVING AT HER
WEDDING TO NICKY
HILTON IN 1950

IMMERSE YOURSELF IN THE DREAM OF COUTURE, ALLOW YOURSELF TO DREAM THE BIGGER DREAM.

}

J'Aton Couture

DAY by DAY

Why I love dressing down

We can never look perfect all the time, but we can dream and sometimes give it a try!

I think the most important thing to consider when you're pulling together pieces for your everyday wardrobe is that they are practical for your lifestyle, but also that they fit your personality and you feel like yourself when you're wearing them. In a perfect world, your wardrobe will be flexible enough to allow you to transition seamlessly from home to work, and day to night.

THE BUILDING BLOCKS OF MY WARDROBE

My Top 10 wardrobe staples

I'm a mum, and I work and I live between two different hemispheres, so life gets busy! Personally, I want to be able to dress my clothes up or down with just the shrug of a coat, the dazzle of a necklace or the tweak of a pair of earrings.

I know that's not everybody's style. There are a lot of girls out there who like to keep their day pieces, their work pieces and their evening pieces separate and who wouldn't dream of going out for the evening without heading home, redoing their hair and make-up and putting on a different outfit.

That's why it's so important to take your lifestyle into account when you're selecting pieces for a capsule wardrobe. The principles behind each item are the same – it's the way you interpret them that imbues them with your style.

1 THE CLASSIC T-SHIRT

The days where a t-shirt was something you borrowed from your boyfriend's wardrobe are long gone. Fitted, slouchy or swing, off the shoulder, round or v-neck, there is a t-shirt cut, neckline and hemline to suit every figure – try a few to find a style that flatters.

White is a good, basic colour with jeans, and a pretty coloured t-shirt can inject a touch of femininity to a work suit. American high-street chain J. Crew uses good-quality fabrics and I like its sizing. C and C California stocks good-quality basics in a rainbow of colours, and I love the vintage look and feel of LA-based KRMA (Kangaroos Roam Mainland Australia) t-shirts. They feel like old, worn-in favourites from the moment you put them on.

Invest in a good-quality T-SHIRT BRA. Clingy t-shirt fabric can be unforgiving, so choose a bra that enhances your curves but gives you a smooth silhouette and, if you're wearing white, stick to a flesh-coloured bra to minimise show-through.

Find a t-shirt shape to suit you

- **LARGE BUST:** If you are well endowed opt for a deep round or deep v-neck t-shirt.

- **SMALL BUST:** If you have a small bust you can carry off a higher neckline, but make sure it doesn't swamp your shape. Go for something feminine that shows your collarbones. If you've got lovely toned arms, try rolling up your sleeves a couple of times to add some detail to the look.

- **BIG ARMS:** If your upper arms lack tone, choose a sleeve that ends just around your elbow. Keeping your forearms visible will keep the look flattering and feminine.

- **IF YOU HAVE A BOYISH FIGURE:** If you're straight up-and-down at the waist, or have a muffin top you want to hide, go for an 'A' line t-shirt that fits at the bust and then flares out. This style will cling to the bits you want people to look at and cover up the rest.

2 THE JEANS

I love layering skinny jeans with boots and a funky t-shirt, a cute jacket and scarf for travelling to photo shoots and television sets, or pottering around the shops and cafés of Marylebone Village.

GOING CASUAL IN ZARA TOP AND JEANS

TIPS and TRICKS for finding a style that suits

- **IF YOUR BODY IS ATHLETIC OR STRAIGHT UP-AND-DOWN,** create a waist with jeans that cinch you in at the middle, smoothing out muffin top and any tummy.

- **IF YOU HAVE CURVY THIGHS,** steer clear of overly faded denim. Trade pale, washed-out and grey shades for indigo or black denim and choose a straight-legged style for an ultra-slimming look.

- **IF YOUR LEGS ARE ON THE SKINNY SIDE,** don't swamp your fabulous pins in jeans that don't fit properly – flaunt them in a stretch legging-fit and chunk up your look with ankle boots. If stretch denim isn't your thing, find a wide-legged, high-waisted pair that fits you snugly around the middle and flares out, 70s-style.

- **IF YOU ARE PETITE,** it's always good to go for a cropped ankle and a higher waist to create the illusion of longer legs. Maximise the effect by accessorising with nude or tan heels. Personally, I love neat, skinny jeans that I can tuck into boots or a European cut I can wear with ballet flats or flip-flops.

JEAN GENIE

Ask most women and they'll say shopping for jeans is their worst nightmare. You'd think the vast selection out there would make it a breeze, but sometimes I think the variety of cuts and colours makes it harder to choose. Here are my tips:

- **LOOK FOR JEANS WITH A WELL-FITTING WAISTBAND**

I don't know anyone who's a fan of the muffin top. You can make yourself look a whole size smaller if you wear well-fitting jeans instead of going for a size too small or a too-tight waistband.

- **CHOOSE YOUR COLOUR WISELY**

Dark colours – indigo blue and black – look crisp, smart and are easy to dress up. To genuinely look smart/casual in faded or ripped jeans, I think you need to invest in a designer pair. Otherwise they simply look old.

- **I LIKE LIGHT-COLOURED DENIM WHEN I'M ON HOLIDAY**

White, pale blue and grey are all beautiful colours for warmer weather.

- **SEEK OUT BRANDS THAT RETAIN THEIR COLOUR AND SHAPE AFTER YOU'VE WASHED THEM**

Lee is a favourite brand because, no matter how much you wash them, the colour doesn't fade and they don't stretch or go baggy. Aussie label Nobody is another reliable brand – it's available online in the UK at my-wardrobe.com.

- **FIND YOUR FIT**

If you're not sure what style suits you, there is help at hand from Ilovejeans.com, a UK-based website dedicated to uniting you with your denim soulmate.

YOU REALLY CAN MAKE YOURSELF LOOK A WHOLE SIZE SMALLER IF YOU WEAR WELL-FITTING JEANS... IT'S TRUE!

Ilovejeans.com offers advice on cuts and brands to suit different body types, and even has a 'Denim Stylist' service in London where you can consult one-to-one with an expert to find your dream jeans. Team up with a girlfriend and book the VIP service to enjoy Champagne and cupcakes during your style session!

Selfridges' Bodymetrics: If you're in London, Selfridges on Oxford Street uses a body scanner to match your body shape with one of three jeans shapes. The scanner takes more than 200 measurements in the blink of an eye and, if you can't find anything in stock, they will customise a pair to fit you like a glove.

Levi's Curve ID: Levi's stores all over the country offer a 'Curve ID' digital fitting service to help you find your dream fit. Can't get to a Levi's store? Take the clever, animated online quiz or follow the simple step-by-step video that shows you how to take your own measurements.

3 THE DAY DRESS

The day dresses I love are light, comfortable, easy to dress up or down and look good if it gets chilly and I have to throw a jacket or pashmina over them.

A great little day dress is not always easy to find. That's why Tabitha and I have designed a whole range of easy-to-wear day dresses for PROJECT D. They work for everything from meetings to lunches, for work or for play.

D&G DRESS BY DOLCE&GABBANA,
SHOES BY CHRISTIAN LOUBOUTIN

INVEST IN QUALITY PIECES that cost a little bit more. They will wash well, and retain their shape and colour. Ideally, select items that you can care for at home – dry cleaning is costly and can be inconvenient.

4 THE SUIT

When you're dressing for business you want to be professional while retaining your own personal style. I don't wear suits often, so I did some serious research before I bought one – a timeless black Dolce&Gabbana jacket and pants with velvet lapels. Mum has a beautiful cream Dolce&Gabbana suit and I kept seeing pictures of their pieces in magazines, so I just went for it and splurged. If you're wearing suits every day for work, you would probably want to have two or three so you can chop and change. Buying a jacket with matching pieces maximises the versatility of your work clothes.

5 THE COAT

A coat is potentially one of the most expensive pieces you will ever purchase, so above all it should be functional. That means warm, and it means a cut and shape that suits you and goes with as many other pieces in your wardrobe as possible. My advice is to steer away from anything too wacky or trend-led unless you're talking a 'classic' trend like military style that comes back season after season and still looks as good today as it did years ago. My favourite, a red cashmere Valentino coat, was expensive, but I've worn it regularly. It has given me 13 great years already – I just have to keep any pesky moths at bay!

6 THE JACKET

Like a coat, a jacket can be a big investment, so it's worth searching out something that's stylish and functional. A good, lightweight jacket will go with everything from a little summer dress to jeans and boots, and will be roomy enough to pop some layers underneath it when the weather gets cold.

My favourite is a cute little cropped leather number from Aussie designer Lisa Ho. I call it my travel jacket, because it's perfect for plane journeys and versatile enough to dress up a smart/casual outfit. For something a little more edgy, I love the girly detailing in KRMA's leather jackets with their cute puff sleeves and lush linings. LA-based Aussie designer Nicholas Bowes has designed stage outfits for Pink, and singers Alicia Keyes and Fergie have been photographed wearing his pieces.

▲

I LOVE MY
PROJECT D COAT
(ABOVE RIGHT)
AND MY
FAVOURITE
JACKETS

{ *A CLASSIC TREND LIKE MILITARY STYLE COMES BACK SEASON AFTER SEASON, AND STILL LOOKS AS GOOD TODAY AS IT DID YEARS AGO.*

7 THE LONG CARDIGAN/PONCHO

Great for a lazy weekend, entertaining at home or maternity wear, a long cardigan or poncho is perfect teamed with jeans or leggings and is super cosy with a pair of Ugg boots. You can style them up differently to achieve different looks. My white Marks & Spencer poncho-style wrap is a real favourite. I wore it throughout my pregnancy, and always take it along to photo shoots to throw over me when I get cold between takes.

8 THE CAPRI PANT

With the right shoe I can do a narrow-fitting, three-quarter length Capri pant. I love J. Crew weekender pants rolled up with a white t-shirt, a wedge heel and a pair of oversized sunglasses – the look is very Sarah Jessica Parker in *Sex and the City*. It's comfortable and stylish enough for entertaining at home or a lazy weekend lunch.

LOVE IT

▶

MAXI POWER: IN AN
ANIMAL-PRINT MAXI
(RIGHT) AND WEARING
A FAB RED MAXI
(FAR RIGHT) IN 2010
AT THE AUSTRALIAN
LAUNCH OF MY
AUTOBIOGRAPHY,
MY STORY

9 THE MAXI DRESS

Perfect for evening entertaining at home
or floating around a barbecue with a jug
of Pimm's in hand, the maxi dress is the
ultimate in comfort dressing. If you're having people
over for dinner – and are in and out of the kitchen
preparing dishes, serving up food and putting things
in the sink – my top tip is not to wear draping sleeves
or they'll be wet and sudsy by the end of the evening.
I like to wear my maxi dresses with über-high heels at
night or with bejewelled flip-flops for a day event.

WEARING A DRESS BY MARTIN GRANT
(LEFT), AND AUDREY HEPBURN (RIGHT)
AS HOLLY GOLIGHTLY IN THE 1961
FILM CLASSIC *BREAKFAST AT TIFFANY'S*.
SHE WEARS AN LBD BY GIVENCHY,
LATER SOLD AT AUCTION FOR £467,200

10 THE LITTLE BLACK DRESS

When I think of an LBD I think of Audrey Hepburn in *Breakfast at Tiffany's*, and that iconic image of the dress with the low-cut back and the string of pearls draping down. LBD perfection! A well-chosen LBD can last for seasons. Basic black is chameleon-like, and can be transformed with the clever use of silver or gold jewellery, a colourful scarf or a statement clutch and shoes. Yves Saint Laurent's little black dresses are timeless and I have a sexy corseted black lace Dolce&Gabbana with a pencil skirt that falls below the knee – very *La Dolce Vita* and crazy beautiful.

TIP

TIPS and TRICKS for a clever wardrobe

YOU DON'T NEED A VAST WARDROBE, JUST A CLEVER WARDROBE. *Breakfast at Tiffany's* provides the perfect template for a capsule wardrobe. You don't get the impression Holly Golightly had an extensive wardrobe, but she had carefully selected investment pieces, styled them up beautifully and wore them whether she was walking to the corner shop or dining in a fancy restaurant. True style.

BUYING VINTAGE

While I've worn some spectacular vintage dresses on the red carpet, I don't wear a lot of vintage day wear. I think if you wear vintage top to toe, there's a risk you'll look like you stepped out of a different era, but I do think one or two original pieces can give an outfit texture, creating a beguiling contrast between old and new.

WHAT GOES AROUND, COMES AROUND

Some people love trawling through vintage shops, but I can't stand that 'vintage' smell. I like places I can shop where they've done the trawling, edited their stock down to good-condition pieces – and cleaned them – before they put them on display.

IN STORE

Atelier Mayer in London is one of my favourite vintage boutiques. They research the provenance of each piece so you know it's authentic, not just vintage-looking.

Project D's
Vivienne dress

ATELIER-MAYER.COM

LOVE IT

VINTAGE

ONLINE VINTAGE

If you're not a fan of going to vintage stores, there is a whole cyberverse of vintage fashion online. You can view pieces by size, era or style, and most sites will give a refund if your purchases don't fit. Some of my favourite online vintage sites are myvintage.co.uk, candysays.co.uk, marthascloset.co.uk and rockit.co.uk.

TAKING INSPIRATION

I love the attention to detail and craftsmanship in vintage fashion, and sometimes Tabs and I will buy pieces for inspiration. Sometimes it's nice to pay homage to past eras in our PROJECT D designs and use features like pin tucks, sunray pleats and smocking, and give them a modern twist.

BEST ONLINE VINTAGE PURCHASE

I found a great little Jean Allen dress on the 1950s specialist vintage site natashabailie.com that I knew would look hot on Tabs. It only cost about £40, and I felt she had to have it before someone else got it, so I sent her the link. It looked brilliant on her and we also used it as inspiration for 'Vivienne' from PROJECT D's Spring/Summer 2011 collection.

BABY...
& BEYOND

My capsule maternity wardrobe

I've streamlined my own wardrobe dramatically since I became a mum. These days what I wear revolves around looking after my son, so my wardrobe is filled with pieces that are easy to throw on, change and wash, and fabrics that disguise little mishaps. In the past I've tended to wear plain pieces, but patterned fabric holds a strange fascination for me all of a sudden.

I've even had to invest in some (whisper it) flat shoes! I have years of running around after Ethan ahead of me and know the heels I used to live in are now reserved for work and occasions where there isn't a baby on board. We're talking uncharted territory here!

 ## Loving my bump

I loved being pregnant and I was very comfortable with the changes to my body throughout my pregnancy. I can remember thinking, 'Wow, I'm going to enjoy this', and relishing the opportunity to wear different things. For my maternity wardrobe I wanted practical, functional and stylish pieces. It's really important to hang on to your style during pregnancy. You've got to feel like yourself or you can lose your identity. Don't invest a fortune in maternity gear. Family and friends gave me lots of stuff, but I really only wore a few pieces. Pick a colour palette and build your maternity wardrobe around it so you can mix and match, just changing the look with beautiful scarves. There's so much choice in maternity wear and many regular styles can double up as maternity clothes, so it's easy to find pieces that work for pregnancy.

The denim

I had no problem wearing maternity jeans (though I know some girls refuse to wear them). I felt comfortable in them and, from the waistband down (which is all anyone ever sees), they looked like regular jeans. My Sweet Belly Couture jeans had a cotton Lycra bellyband stitched above the waistband, and I wore a lot of Mamas and Papas jeans with elasticated side panels that stretched with the bump.

PHOTOGRAPHED
BY DAVID GUBERT
IN 2010

Many regular brands have maternity lines. I had Paige maternity jeans that looked like they had a normal waistband but had buttons and elasticated tabs so I could make adjustments as my bump grew. I had some J Brand maternity jeans with stretchy panels and lived in my black Seraphine jeans, which had a little pocket for my belly.

When I fell pregnant, I gave away most of my jeans. I wanted someone to enjoy them and can remember thinking, 'I'm never going to fit back into those'. Oddly, the reverse happened and, once I'd had Ethan, I was actually smaller than I was before. I had to run out and buy new jeans. US brand J. Crew do sizing that works really well for me. Now I just go to their website and order online when I need a new pair of jeans.

The underwear

There's so much variety now, you don't have to wear daggy underwear while you're pregnant. If you're going to buy one feeding bra, make it a Bravado. I loved mine for its softness. It didn't cut in or rub and was really easy to wear.

For dressy occasions, I couldn't have got by without my Elle Macpherson maternity bra. It is low cut and lacy, and went under everything. Maternity Spanx look really ugly, but I had to do red carpets and go to events, and they gave me a smooth line underneath my dresses. And if you are a girl who won't leave the house unless your underwear matches, it's worth checking out HOT Milk's range of sexy lingerie.

PHOTOGRAPHED BY DAVID GUBERT IN 2010

{ *I LOVED BEING PREGNANT AND I REMEMBER THINKING: 'WOW, I'M GOING TO ENJOY THIS.'*

PHOTOGRAPHED BY DAVID GUBERT IN 2010

DAY BY DAY: *MY STYLE*

The bellyband

Bellybands look a little bizarre, but they're amazingly effective. You pop one around your waist and under your tummy, and it just holds the weight of your bump. They're great if you're on your feet all day.

The hosiery

Once you have a bump, normal tights and pantyhose cut into you around the middle. I had maternity opaques that came up higher at the front from Mothercare, and I'd wear them with a dress and boots.

The black pants

I wore my Slacks & Co black maternity pants all the time. They're very chic and although they have stretchy side panelling they're not overtly maternity. I'd dress them up with a nice shirt and a tuxedo jacket to look smart for meetings and pop a sparkly top over them when I was going out.

The cover-up

Sometimes when I was out walking I felt a little bit exposed, and wanted to be a bit protective of my bump and cover it up. I had long cardigans that weren't specifically maternity that looked great layered over a t-shirt and bellyband, and an amazing Stephanie Schell poncho, which you can style eight different ways and is also reversible.

The shirt

I looked for tops that would work while I was pregnant and afterwards, with stretchy fabrics, ruching, hidden panels for feeding and long hemlines. My long,

{ I looked for TOPS that would
work while I was pregnant and
afterwards, with stretchy fabrics
and hidden panels for feeding. }

stretchy Metalicus top was an easy-care staple – I could chuck it in the washing machine and it didn't crush when I packed it.

My Ripe maternity shirt was very comfortable because the wrap-top shape expanded as my belly grew. Melissa Odabash makes great feather-light popover tops, perfect for summer pregnancies over a maternity tank and jeans. When I was in Australia I lived in mine.

The feeding top

I had a few little white Mothercare feeding tops I could wear underneath anything. Because I had a C-section, I wanted something that would hold me firmly after the birth that wasn't going to rub on the scar. They have a double layer of fabric, so they provide a protective layer when your stomach is feeling all jelly-like after you've given birth.

The swimwear

Swimming is great when you're pregnant, because the water helps take the weight off your belly. I didn't always swim laps – I would often just walk in the shallow end of the pool. The resistance was good exercise and my osteopath recommended it when I had a sore back. I bought some regular Marks & Spencer bikinis. It sells tops and bottoms separately so you can mix and match sizes.

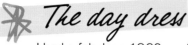 The day dress

I had a fabulous 1960s-cut lace dress with gorgeous sleeves from EGG, a New Zealand maternity label, that I'd throw over a tank top with tights, boots and a scarf or wear as a long top over jeans. It worked for day or night, and I could crumple it up in a suitcase and it didn't need ironing. If I could only choose one maternity dress it would be that one.

PROJECT D's 'Royal Flush' in pebble (far right) is a flattering cut. I wore it while I was pregnant with Ethan and it can be styled to suit a business meeting or a lunch with the girls. I remember wearing it to meet Jo Elvin, the editor of *Glamour* magazine, when we were talking about me writing a monthly column and I felt confident but relaxed wearing it – and I got the gig!

Sydney designer Stephanie Schell's designs are ingenious, beautiful and functional pieces that accommodate your belly with hidden zips under the arms either side of the bodice, so it's easy to get in and out for breastfeeding.

With dresses you don't always have to opt for maternity wear. I had a lovely bias-cut empire line dress by Australian designer Yeojin Bae that was very flattering. I wore it for day and night, before and after the birth.

The evening dress

We were due to launch PROJECT D at Selfridges in 2010 and, because of the volcanic ash cloud that grounded air traffic, most of our dresses were stuck in transit. Luckily we had this black, sequined stretchy number, 'Casino', in my size or I would have had nothing to wear that night. You'd never think the elements of this dress – tight-fitting, sequin-covered, stretchy Lycra – would suit a heavily pregnant woman. It's a little optical illusion that makes this dress work. The

asymmetric neckline really elongates the body and can slim down a heavy bust, whether or not you're pregnant. It was perfect for my capsule maternity wardrobe because it just stretched around me as I grew.

WEARING PROJECT D 'CASINO'
AT THE SELFRIDGES LAUNCH
OF OUR LABEL (LEFT); IN PROJECT
D'S 'ROYAL FLUSH' DRESS (ABOVE)
WITH PROJECT D MODEL, KIM, AND
MY BUSINESS PARTNER TABITHA
WEARING PROJECT D 'POKER'

In bloom

This photograph was taken by one of my favourite Australian photographers, Chris Colls. When we were planning the cover shoot we were conscious that I would be heavily pregnant and we wanted to make a feature of the bump. There was no way I was stripping off Demi Moore-style with my hands not quite covering my bits and pieces, so we went for this flowing Aurelio Costarella dress.

Until you've been pregnant you never really understand what people mean when they say they feel like they are blooming, but that's exactly how I felt at the time, and I think this photograph conveys that blossoming emotion perfectly.

PHOTOGRAPHED BY CHRIS COLLS FOR THE COVER OF *WHO* MAGAZINE AUSTRALIA, APRIL 2010

LOVE my LABEL

How Tabitha and I
started PROJECT D

I launched my very own fashion label – PROJECT D – with my best friend Tabitha Somerset Webb in April 2010.

Now several collections in, we know we're nowhere near having 'made it'. We're still a little private company up against the big fashion labels – there's no corporation backing us. We're still the girls who eat cupcakes, love Champagne and design dresses we love, and that we hope you'll love too. We've said to our customers, buyers and the press: we're in this for the long haul if you are. We really want to be there and be a label you can rely on. We have a long-term commitment to our label – it's our passion!

WEARING PROJECT D, PHOTOGRAPHED BY GEORGES ANTONI FOR *WHO* MAGAZINE, MAY 2011

Bagging myself
a business partner

I was a big fan of Tabs' luxury handbag brand Tabitha and called her up to introduce myself. It turned out her design studio was close to where I lived in Battersea, so I popped around to say hello and see her whole collection. Throughout my life there have been just a few people I have had an instant connection with, and Tabs was one of them. Within 10 minutes of walking in the door and chatting to her I'd announced: 'We're going to be really good friends.' Did I really say that aloud, I wondered to myself?

Lots of long lunches, power walks and girls' nights out followed. Occasionally we talked about ways we could work together, but it wasn't until six years later, walking our favourite route along the Thames in Battersea, that my mouth got the better of me again. 'Why don't we do a clothing line together?' I blurted out, ready to pass it off as a joke if she was horrified by the idea.

It was a little far-fetched, because neither of us had done a fashion collection like this before. Happily, she managed to see beyond the crazy and agreed. I didn't have to use my 'graceful' exit strategy, and the seeds of PROJECT D were sown.

PHOTOGRAPHED BY ELISABETH HOFF FOR PROJECT D

{ I wanted to build a LABEL
with my friend – something we
could be proud of. I knew it
would take time and energy, but
that would mean we got to spend
a lot of time together. }

After that, things started happening fast. Tabs called me to tell me she had
some investors interested, which made everything feel very real. It didn't take
long for me to understand what entrepreneurs mean when they say if they'd
known what was involved in starting their own business, they never would have
taken it on. But that great, blind – 'Whoo, hooo, we're going to have our own
clothing label!' – ignorance definitely got us through the initial set-up.

We agreed that whether PROJECT D took off or not, we'd stay friends. It was a risk. I've seen friendships fall apart in the face of success as well as failure. Both have the power to change lives and split people up. So holding on to our friendship has always been our number one focus. You only have to watch *Style Queen* to know that business has its good days and bad days, and PROJECT D has already experienced its fair share of dramas (thanks to volcanic ash clouds, missing couriers and the nine-hour-plus time difference between London and Melbourne), but the laughs we have together help us ride those waves.

> *OUR BEST BUSINESS TOOL IS TO LAUGH WHEN THINGS FEEL OVERWHELMING. IT GIVES US THE ENERGY TO FIND A SOLUTION.*

The PROJECT D philosophy

We want to design beautiful pieces for real women – stylish dresses that do the work for you. Our aim is to design pieces that suit everyone from 23-year-olds to funky 65-year-old mums and grandmas, and range from day, to cocktail, to evening wear. Our personal styles may differ – I'm into timeless classics, Tabs is more rock 'n' roll – but neither of us is into fad fashions. If something in our collection happens to channel the catwalk buzz, that's great, but we're not trying to be on-trend with everything we create. Our priorities are femininity, fit and fabulous detail. We want the women who buy our dresses to come back to us again and again because they love the dresses, know what they're going to get and trust us.

IN PROJECT D
'POKER' DRESS

The PROJECT D chemistry

Tabs and I don't just have different personal styles, we also have different working styles. I'm all about order and organisation, and I *love* a list. Tabs' style is, how shall I put this, a little more *'freeform'*.

If you watched *Style Queen* you'll have seen me – very reluctantly – part with my 'Style Bible' of cuttings and shed a few tears before heading back to Australia to have Ethan. I haven't had it back from Tabs, and there's every chance it's still buried somewhere on her desk in the PROJECT D offices – a desk that gives me palpitations every time I look at it.

In spite of our differences, we seem to really come alive when we combine our forces.

Tabs is in love with Dolly Parton, and inspired by pink gingham and 'Dollywood'. I like to draw on old Hollywood glamour with a modern twist. It's where we clash that the magic begins.

The first PROJECT D collection (Autumn/Winter 2010) was born out of a crazy brainstorming session (and a bottle of wine) at Tabs' kitchen table. The most important thing we learned that night was that our sketching skills are non-existent! Tabs' sketches looked like gingerbread men, and mine looked like badly executed toast cut-outs. With hours of hard work, and patterns made and cut to our every specification, we were bowled over by what we achieved for our first collection.

We both do the creatives for the clothing design – it's our favourite bit. Tabs runs the day-to-day business, we both do PR for the brand and I put sticky notes scribbled with ideas on everything that doesn't move, which reduces Tabs to fits of laughter.

We start with a dress shape we love, a fabric swatch that inspires us or glamorous vintage pictures. We put a lot of time into making each design both beautiful and practical. Sometimes we work in the office, but more often than not our best work is done over a home-cooked meal and a glass of wine.

Because I've divided my time between Melbourne and London since we created our first collection, when we can't get together for formal concept meetings we email each other links to things we've seen online, and snippets of inspiration from magazines and the fashion history books we both love. We're constantly throwing forward ideas – here, there and everywhere.

{ IT'S WHERE WE CLASH THAT THE MAGIC BEGINS.

◀ I LOVE A
SPRITZ OF
PROJECT D'S
FRAGRANCE

The yummy smell of success

Concocting our signature fragrance was girly heaven.
I never feel dressed unless I've spritzed myself with scent,
so the chance to create our dream perfume was one of
my highlights of our PROJECT D adventure so far.

Our signature scent has top notes of neroli, bergamot and ylang ylang; heart
notes of tuberose, Japanese osmanthus, mimosa and purple orchid, and base
notes of sandalwood, saffron, musks and amber.

The inspiration for our set of three purse sprays came from our working lives.
Because we're so busy, Tabs and I are both big fans of any outfit that can be
updated from day to night with a few carefully placed accessories. We wanted
to see if we could carry that concept through to a perfume, breaking down our
signature fragrance into its component parts (which we christened **Dawn**, **Day**
and **Dusk**) to carry the wearer through from morning to night.

What PROJECT D has taught me...

Don't panic, it's just pattern! When I was younger I almost completely avoided patterned and printed fabrics. I felt swamped by them – like they were wearing me rather than me wearing them.

PROJECT D has taught me that it's all about finding patterns I do like. Tabs uses patterns boldly and gives them a modern twist, which I love. Like me, she loves her fashion history, and Helen O'Neill's book, *Florence Broadhurst: Her Secret & Extraordinary Lives*, about Australia's most famous textile and wallpaper designer, has been a huge source of inspiration for both of us.

IT'S OKAY TO BREAK YOUR STYLE RULES

I always used to avoid wearing short hemlines – I used to be self-conscious about my legs, and shorter styles aren't always the best when you're trying to elongate the body. But since I've had Ethan, I've found myself rocking shorter styles more often. Tabs and I joke that, as I'm approaching 40, I'm hitting my midlife crisis. It's either the short skirts or I'd be out buying myself a red Ferrari! This photo of us, which is above next to some of our sketches, makes me laugh, because Tabs has always been the rock chick and I've always gone for the old Hollywood style. We looked at one another on the way to the *Style Queen*

launch in Sydney (February 2011) and it was like a moment from the movie *Freaky Friday*. I was dressed like her and she was dressed like me! They say the people you hang out with can influence your style, and here's the proof.

STYLE IS IN THE DETAIL

It's the finishing touches that transform a garment from okay to amazing. Small alterations – a raised hemline here, a tweaked neckline there – can help you make more of any outfit. Replace the buttons to add a unique twist to a basic blazer. Give an old favourite a facelift with fabric dye. Add a personal twist to a high-street item with the judicious use of ribbon, sequins, lace… The only limit is your imagination. If you don't feel confident making customisations yourself, call on your local tailor or seamstress for expert help.

THE HIGHER THE HAIR

Style isn't just about wearing the right dress, it's about the entire ensemble: the hair, the make-up, the shoes, bag and accessories. Okay, big hair might not always be the answer, but a well-thought-out do and carefully selected accessories are the finishing touches that cement your look.

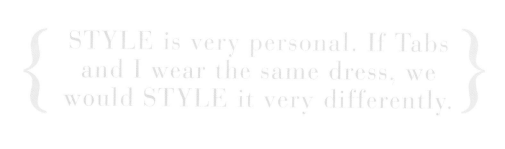

{ STYLE is very personal. If Tabs and I wear the same dress, we would STYLE it very differently. }

THERE'S A PLACE FOR PINK GINGHAM IN COUTURE

Tabs' obsession with all things country music means I have to accept that pink gingham will make an appearance in a PROJECT D collection at some stage. It's only a matter of time until line-dancing marathons and Dolly and Kenny tribute shows just don't cut it any more, and pink-and-white check makes its catwalk debut for PROJECT D!

THE BUSINESS SIDE OF FASHION IS AS IMPORTANT AS DESIGN

I've learnt to look at each dress with an aesthetic eye and a business eye. Each piece needs to be something I both love, and would love to wear, and something that will really work for women on a functional level.

THIS TIME IT'S PERSONAL

Style is very personal. If Tabs and I were to wear the same dress, we would style it differently. I prefer simple and classic — Tabs goes for relaxed and racy.

MY SISTER, KYLIE

When I showed Kylie our first 'look book', I was holding my breath hoping for a good reaction. I was over the moon when she not only liked our dresses, but also started picking out ones for her wardrobe. I never show her anything until I feel it's perfect.

GETTING TO GRIPS WITH PATTERN AND PRINT FOR PROJECT D

Mini Me-nogue

I'm always saying I need a clone, and I'm only half joking! I was working on a dress with Ralph & Russo in 2008, and I was so busy with *The X Factor* that I was having difficulty finding time for all the fittings, so Tamara (Ralph) tracked down a company in Paris and we commissioned them to make a mannequin to my exact body shape.

THE MAKING OF THE MANNEQUIN

I was photographed in a Lycra catsuit from every angle, then had all my measurements taken. All that information was sent away and an almost perfect replica came back, complete with arms and legs. The attention to detail was incredible. A few more measurements and some tweaking, and I had an identical twin, complete with my name emblazoned across her chest.

These days my 'Dannii-Manni' lives in the PROJECT D offices, and if I can't be there for a fitting, she steps in (on her meticulously stuffed legs) and does the honours. My shape has changed a little since Ethan was born – my booty isn't quite so big and I'm smaller around the waist – but they can put a dress on 'her' and roughly know how it's going to fit on me.

PROJECT D – Next?

In the entertainment industry, you're only as good as your last performance. In fashion, you're only as good as your last collection. Tabs and I know we have to keep improving, and we're ready to work our socks off to do it.

Eventually we'd like to be a lifestyle brand, with a collection of clothes, bags, perfume and shoes. I think people really identify with us as friends who love Champagne and cupcakes and having a giggle together. We're constantly getting customer requests for men's, baby and bridal ranges – and of course it would be great to expand – but we're not about to compromise quality in the process. It has to be a gradual evolution.

{ The very first CELEBRITY picture we saw was Elizabeth Hurley wearing our zebra-print dress. It was such a thrilling, fashion landmark moment! }

Tabitha

{

EACH PIECE NEEDS TO BE SOMETHING I BOTH LOVE AND WOULD LOVE TO WEAR.

WEARING THE PROJECT D 'MONACO' DRESS,
PHOTOGRAPHED BY GEORGES ANTONI FOR
WHO MAGAZINE, MAY 2011

164

Me in Project D

I wore PROJECT D 'Q' from our James Bond-inspired Spring/
Summer 2011 collection to PROJECT D's catwalk debut in
Sydney in February 2011. It's actually a top you can wear to
the beach with flip-flops or with jeans, but it's so slinky I was
dying to wear it as a dress with heels. It's shorter than I would
normally wear, but the asymmetric hemline and v-neck help
to elongate my body.

LOVE the LOT

Shoes, bags, baubles, bangles
and bright shiny beads

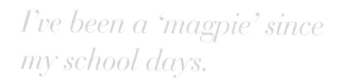

I've been a 'magpie' since my school days.

From sneaking a bangle into the classroom, my friends and I would gradually add more and more accessories to the point where our uniforms were so heavily adorned that we'd rattle. It was our first opportunity to choose our own stuff and express ourselves. The headmaster would make us remove our treasures, but it was never long before the cycle started all over again, and we'd be adding little embellishments here and there.

STEPHEN WEBSTER JEWELS ADD A FABULOUS DAZZLE TO A DOLCE&GABBANA TULLE CORSET DRESS

THE PRINCIPLES

(BEHIND MY ACCESSORIES COLLECTION)

I believe a beautiful outfit doesn't truly come alive until it's been accessorised. I still have accessories I bought years and years ago, and my collection is an eclectic mix of big statement and small elegant pieces. Accessory choices are influenced by lifestyle: if you need to know the time, you wear a watch. I love earrings, but I don't wear them much at home these days because Ethan tends to grab at them. Then you have the accessories that are so much a part of your personality that you feel naked without them – an heirloom handed down to you or a good-luck charm.

You can completely change the personality of an outfit by styling it up with different accessories, and you don't have to spend a fortune to create your own unique look.

I often ask friends about a fabulous piece they're wearing and it will turn out it's from a high street store. It's all about being clever, and mix-and-matching those pieces so they work together and make you feel fantastic.

A BESPOKE 'EBURY' BAG BY ANYA HINDMARCH, CLUTCH BAG BY YVES SAINT LAURENT, AND SHOES BY SERGIO ROSSI AND DOLCE&GABBANA

MANOLO B

The bags

THE DAY BAG

I like a decent-sized bag so I can throw everything in it. I joke that my handbag is a mini-wardrobe. I choose bags with at least one zippered pocket inside them where I can keep the things I don't want to lose – my keys, phone and lip balm. I put everything else in a Ruby and Ginger handbag insert, and just lift it out to transfer my gear to another bag. It's a little piece of portable genius.

THE CLUTCH BAG

There's so much opportunity to express yourself with a clutch bag. I have a gold leather Lulu Guinness bag in the shape of a pair of lips that is a personal favourite. My Giani Bernini clutch has a detachable strap, so I can pop it under my arm or hang it over my shoulder to keep my hands free for a glass of Champagne, introductions and to help myself to nibbles at a wedding or cocktail reception.

When you're not using your CLUTCH BAGS, stuff them to help them keep their shape. I really like to use bubble wrap because it has some guts to it and won't mark or stain the inside of the bag.

A LACE DRESS BY DOLCE&GABBANA AND 'EBURY' BAG BY ANYA HINDMARCH

THE BAG BRANDS

Tabitha

Without Tabitha bags there might never have been a PROJECT D!
Tabs' luxury handbag designs were a favourite of mine long before we joined
forces on our own fashion label. I love the lush-coloured leather and amazing
embellishments Tabitha uses in her bags. They're big, slouchy and made for
carting around my many essentials, yet still manage to look fab at the same
time. I often say to her that they look good enough to eat.

Kara Ross

Exquisite evening clutch bags with semi-precious stones on them. I have two
and plan to keep adding to them – I want a whole collection!

Anya Hindmarch

My sister Kylie gave me my most treasured handbag, an Anya Hindmarch
bespoke 'Ebury'. It has a special handwritten message from her, printed in gold
just inside the bag, which says…

'little and big sisters… always xx'

It's a timeless classic that will make a family heirloom one day!

KYLIE'S GIFT: A BESPOKE 'EBURY' BAG BY ANYA HINDMARCH

The scarves

I feel naked if I leave the house without a scarf, like the Tabitha scarf I'm wearing in these photos. I'm constantly looking out for new ones and thinking about ways to pair scarves with different outfits. Draping a scarf has the power to elongate and slim the body in the same way as vertical stripes and pleats.

To store SCARVES, I hang them on fuzzy hangers, a couple over each, so they're easy to find and don't crease or fall on the floor of my closet.

The tights

I love wearing black opaque tights with little sweater dresses in winter. Seamed stockings are very cheeky with 1950s-style dresses and high stilettos and, as you'll know from my 'Kylie Homecoming' story, I love a 'power' fishnet. There are loads of fine fishnets to choose from, including my 'lock and load' variety, and they look super-glamorous with a pencil skirt.

'Seamed stockings
are very cheeky with
50s-style dresses
and high stilettos'

LOVE IT

'Hats make me happy...'

The hats

THE BOWLER

I've got a gorgeous black bowler hat from a Marks & Spencer commercial we filmed in London. I don't get many opportunities to wear it, but I'm planning to hang it on the corner of the mirror in my wardrobe so I get to enjoy it just the same.

THE BERET

My go-to when I have a bad hair day, the beret hides a multitude of follicular misdeeds when I can't get to grips with one of the dos my hair stylists, Christian and Fotini, have taught me to do myself. I have them in navy and black so they go with just about everything. I love the way they keep my head toasty warm in winter.

*...this one by
Philip Treacy
is a favourite*

THE FEDORA

Gold from Marks & Spencer, worn at an angle to create the illusion of height.

THE DRESSY HAT

Flowers and Philip Treacy! My wardrobe wonderland… How can I choose my favourites? You can never have enough closet space.

The sunglasses

Don't underestimate the power of a pair of sunglasses to jazz up an everyday outfit.

I never go anywhere without a pair in my handbag and a back-up pair in the car, and I have a few spare pairs in a drawer in my closet. I choose them according to my mood. Some pairs are very 'hey, look at me', others allow me to hide away when I'm in the mood to blend into the background, still others are just practical for throwing on when I'm driving or have had a bit of a sleepless night with Ethan.

The secret is finding a shape that suits your face. I think aviators are timeless, and I have gold, silver and a spare pair from Dyrberg/Kern. I own a pair of cherry-red heart-shaped sunnies from Cutler and Gross for rose-coloured moments, and super-sized black frames when I want to amp up the glam factor.

VINTAGE CHRISTIAN DIOR GLASSES
FROM RETROSUN

183

'ABSOLUTELY FABULOUS!'

The shoes

Whether it's on the red carpet or in front of TV cameras, I'm
judged, quite literally, from top to toe. My feet are pretty teensy
– I take a European size 35 shoe – and many brands don't
even make shoes that small, so it can be quite an achievement
for me to find something I like. If I see a shoe I like in my size
and it looks good on my foot and leg, I tend to buy it when
I see it and hope that down the line it goes with a dress. It
means I generally go for more conservative shoes with outfits,
because I don't really have a million to choose from on the day.

FLATS

Tabs and I have been walking to work a lot lately – we've even been known
to run through Sydney to get to appointments on time! We'll wear ballet flats
or flip-flops, race to a meeting, then put on our heels, pop the flats in our
handbags, and attempt to make our grand entrance. Lindsay Phillips makes
cute 'switch flops' and 'snap shoes' – flip-flops and ballet flats that you can
customise yourself.

FLIP-FLOPS

Where I come from, we call flip-flops 'thongs'. I've never been a big fan, because
they are sooooo flat and weren't that comfortable on my crazy stiletto-loving
feet, but since Ethan came along I've had to make some concessions to flat
footwear. Aussie brand Holster makes fantastic embellished jelly flip-flops
with a very slight wedge heel that I live in during the summer (holsteruk.co.uk).

'My feet are pretty teensy...'

GOLD SANDALS
BY ALEXANDER
MCQUEEN.
GOLD SHOES
BY GIUSEPPE
ZANOTTI AND
FLATS BY LANVIN

THE SHOE BRANDS

Giuseppe Zanotti

There are many good reasons why Italy is renowned for its shoemakers and Giuseppe Zanotti is one of them! He creates shoes that are beautiful, and shoes that are beautiful with an edge. I visit the Giuseppe Zanotti store on Walton Street in South Kensington every opportunity I get.

Charlotte Olympia

British shoe designer Charlotte Olympia is amazing. Her handcrafted shoes are pure old Hollywood glamour but she always manages to introduce a modern twist. I have a black satin pair with a really high heel, a platform sole and a frill at the back, and I wear them with practically everything. Her trademark is a nude-coloured sole with a gold metallic spider web branding it. I love the underside of her shoes as much as the shoes themselves.

Georgina Goodman

I discovered British shoemaker Georgina Goodman through her unmistakable 'Love' shoe. Her shoes are just so cool and different. They are beautiful – it wouldn't be a sin to own them in two colourways!

PHOTOGRAPHED BY SEAN MCMENOMY

SOMETIMES THE BOTTOMS OF SHOES CAN LOOK JUST AS AMAZING AS THE TOPS!

Yves Saint Laurent

I'll go into the YSL store on Bond Street for one pair of shoes and come out with a pair in every colour. This may seem excessive, but this is a splurge that has actually worked wonders for photoshoots, the red carpet and TV shows.

Sergio Rossi

Italian shoemaker Sergio Rossi's designs are fantastic, with stack heels, sexy strapping, and divine crystal and metallic embellishments.

SHOES BY
GEORGINA
GOODMAN AND
CHRISTIAN
LOUBOUTIN
(LEFT), AND
SHOES BY SERGIO
ROSSI AND YVES
SAINT LAURENT
(BELOW)

THE BOOT BRANDS

Giuseppe Zanotti

I wanted a good pair of boots, but I didn't want to invest in a pair the wrong length for me. I'm not very tall, so style-wise I tend not to go for too long a boot because it swamps me. I love Giuseppe Zanotti shoes and found a pair of their boots that come to the top of my knee – longer than I'd normally wear, but because they are black and just such a nice, slim cut, they suit me down to the ground (if you'll excuse the pun). I lived in them during winter, running in and out of *The X Factor* filming. I don't know what I'd do if Giuseppe stopped stocking this exact boot. I'd have to track him down and beg him to make them specially for me.

Ozitude Uggs

I'd never wear them outside unless I was heading to a yoga class, but there's nothing yummier than cosying up at home in a pair of Uggs after a long day in stilettos. Ozitude do the bling-iest Uggs around. I have a blue pair with Swarovski crystal anchors on the back, and you can also have them embellished with your initials, crowns, angel wings or cherries. I defy you not to sigh a happy 'ahhhhhh' as you slip your feet into them.

Holster Wellingtons

A pair of gumboots with wedge heels and sparkles so you can see over the crowds at music festivals? Sign me up! Aussie-made Holster wellies are fleece-lined and crystal-encrusted for a little bling while you sing.

PHOTOGRAPHED BY CHRIS CRAYMER IN 2010 FOR UK *GLAMOUR* MAGAZINE

'There's nothing yummier than cosying up at home in a pair of Uggs'

The jewellery

RINGS

Rings are a great way to express yourself. I got to wear some magnificent statement pieces on *The X Factor* – bold, funky, chunky rocks and quirky sparkly cocktail rings. Fashionista heaven. One of my favourite ring designers is Lola Rose. They design with classic-cut crystals and semi-precious stones and a choice of gold and silver that makes their pieces timeless and versatile – I can wear the same big ring with jeans and a jacket or use it to dress up a frock in the evening.

EVERYDAY RINGS

For day wear, simple and delicate is always in style. I'm slowly adding to my collection of Annoushka stackable rings. I can mix the metals and stones to suit my mood. There's a combination to go with every outfit.

GOLD OR SILVER?

I go through phases when I prefer gold or silver so, if I really love a piece, I never give up on it and chuck it out. I know it will come back into favour eventually.

SOMETHING BORROWED

A lot of 'unauthorised borrowing' goes on in the Minogue household, particularly when it comes to accessories. I found a beautiful pearl necklace in my mum's jewellery box a few years ago (far right). The design is classic and the pearls have that wonderful aged sheen, as if they have been polished up with beautiful memories. It's one of fashion's great truisms that if something looks good on your mother, it will look good on you and, happily for me, my lovely mum made the loan permanent!

LOVE IT

{ COCO CHANEL was famous for layering up her pearls and used to mix real pearls with costume pieces to maximise the effect. }

Since I became a mum to Ethan
I've accumulated sentimental pieces.
I have a little NECKLACE with an
'E' on it and another with his name
and birth date engraved on it. It's
nice to have a little keepsake of him
with me when I leave the house.

VINTAGE JEWELLERY

Accessorising with vintage jewellery can create a real talking point. I'm a fan of women wearing antique men's watches. You can pick up fabulous designer pieces at auction for a fraction of the price you'd pay for a new one. If you inherit a piece of jewellery you love, but you don't love it on you, don't leave it languishing in the bottom of your jewellery box. A bit of remodelling can turn a pendant or locket into a funky charm bracelet, and you can create a piece that really speaks to you by having a stone reset. Annina Vogel is renowned for transforming antique gold into contemporary pieces.

ACCESSORY STORAGE

● ACRYLIC RING BOX

Muji's individual ring boxes are great for packing rings when I'm travelling or carrying jewellery options to a studio for a photo shoot or if I want to pop a ring into my handbag wardrobe to take a dress from day to night.

● ACRYLIC JEWELLERY BOX

I use the large Muji jewellery boxes with the pull-out trays for storing jewellery at home so I can see everything at a glance and access it quickly. They're stackable, and you can purchase inserts so that you can configure them in different ways to keep jewellery separated.

MUJI JEWELLERY BOX WITH COCKTAIL RINGS BY LOLA ROSE, A STEPHEN WEBSTER SILVER RING, CHERRY BLOSSOM JEWELS BY SEAN LEANE, DINNY HALL GOLD BRACELETS, AND EARRINGS BY ASTLEY CLARKE AND MONICA VINADER

The necklace

I still have a necklace I bought at Patricia Field's store in New York, long before she was doing the styling on *Sex and the City*.

When I moved to New York to record my first album, I used to walk past her little shop on the way from my apartment to the recording studio. I was only 17, and I was coaxed through the door by all the wonderful treasures in the window. The shop assistants were drag queens and I used to love them, so I was always popping in to say hi. I spotted this thick gold-beaded chain with a crucifix on it and had to have it. If you watch, you'll see I wore it in *Love and Kisses* – the very first video clip of my music career. I've taken the cross off it now, but I still wear the beaded chain all the time.

MY BELOVED NECKLACE
– TREASURED AND
WELL-WORN... STILL!

I love
GETTING
ORGANISED

My wardrobe and packing

There's something I'm really good at – getting organised.

When you're busy it's the only way to keep everything on track. I'm constantly refining my systems for keeping my wardrobe, bathroom cupboards and office in order. Packing is a speciality, learnt years ago when I first started touring. You may think getting ready to go on holiday is such a laborious job, and I can't promise you'll ever love spring cleaning your closet, but by the time you've read this chapter, I hope my tips may make these reviled tasks a little easier. Call me crazy, but I just love getting organised.

PHOTOGRAPHED BY DAVID GUBERT IN 2010

I LOVE GETTING ORGANISED: _MY STYLE_

TRAVEL

Bags, boxes and cases

When it comes to packing, having the right cases and bags is half the battle. Through a process of research, trial and error, I've found a collection of travel tools that works for me.

THE CARRY-ON

Exhaustive research into the perfect cabin bag turned up this little gem – my Louis Vuitton Pegase bag. With airlines increasingly restrictive about the size of cabin baggage, it's a perfect fit for long haul or domestic flights. (Beware: they have different cabin allowances.) It's on the expensive side but some things are well worth the investment. Made of canvas with a durable zip and wheels, it's big enough for my laptop, and I pop in my travel documents in a clear plastic wallet. It's now 10 years old, but still looks brand new.

MY LULU
GUINNESS
SUITCASE
▼

THE SUITCASE

My Samsonite suitcase is 15 years old, and has been around the world with me over and over again. I prefer a hard-shell case – if it comes off a plane into the rain, my packing stays dry, and if the baggage handlers throw it around nothing gets damaged. I have found the clip fastenings on hard cases are more secure than zips on bags – you only need one broken tooth for a whole zip to ping open and reveal all your knickers to the other passengers waiting at the luggage carousel – and its built-in combination lock means I don't have to worry about losing the keys.

THE MAKE-UP BAG

A make-up bag should be functional and glamorous! Make Up Store does make-up bags in a range of sizes in glitzy fabrics that are easy to spot in the deepest, darkest handbag. I always travel with a hanging wash bag. They pack flat, have clear compartments so I can see where everything is and are perfect for hanging on a hotel bathroom door. They're sold at Marks & Spencer, Boots and Superdrug.

THE IN-FLIGHT TOILETRY BAG

Dermot O'Leary bought me a gorgeous Anya Hindmarch toiletry bag for Christmas and I use it to

{ The LOUIS VUITTON Pegase bag is on the expensive side, but some things are well worth the investment.

carry my in-flight essentials. It has one compartment labelled 'take-off' and a second labelled 'touch-down', and I pack it with the little things I like to take on board in clear zip-lock bags and pop them in the two compartments. Beautiful!

THE MAKE-UP BRUSH ROLL

I adore my Ultimate Brush Roll by Aussie celebrity stylist Trudy Joyce. It is compact, packs flat and comes in a rainbow of colours and fabrics. It has lots of compartments so you can organise your brushes and products.

THE MAKE-UP BRUSH TUBE

On a short trip when I don't need my entire brush kit, I use Amy Jean Eye Couture eye collection brush kit — a leather tube with a snap-shut lid.

THE JEWELLERY BOX

Angie Smith, who was my style consultant for *The X Factor*, gave me an Oliver Bonas jewellery box that is perfect for packing rings, bracelets and earrings. The compartments and fastenings stop everything getting jumbled up. I'm also a big fan of fisherman's tackle boxes, which are inexpensive and protect my treasures. I wrap each item in a tissue before dropping it into a compartment to prevent tangles.

THE SHOE BAG

I pop each pair of shoes into a shoe bag to protect them and prevent them from damaging other things in my case. Use shoe trees to stop your shoes getting squashed and put each pair top-to-toe in its bag to save space. Put boots into a drawstring boot bag and stuff gym shoes with 'cedar socks' — fabric shoe stuffers filled with cedar chips — to absorb moisture and smells.

{ It's really important that your
TRAVEL TOOLS work for you. }

THE LINGERIE BAG

Separate your smalls with a 'wash me, wear me' lingerie bag. Clean underwear
goes in the 'wear me' compartment and used underwear goes in the 'wash me'
compartment. It has a strap so you can hang it up in your hotel room, too.

CHARGER STORAGE BAGS

How do you stop your phone charger, camera charger, laptop charger, travel
adaptors and sundry other cables tangling themselves in the bottom of your
suitcase? Get yourself handy little charger bags by Charge Me Up and you'll
never face technological spaghetti again.

Choosing a holiday wardrobe that works for you

It's pretty easy to over-pack when you go on holiday, and it can be so difficult to refine your holiday wardrobe to a practical – and packable – number of clothes. Taking everything is not the answer! Nor is going shopping the moment you touch down because you've got nothing to go with your favourite skirt…

My mum bought me a cheap clothes rail and I use it to help me decide which clothes to pack. For me it's a packing essential, but if it seems like overkill you can easily lay things out on your bed and the floor of your bedroom.

First, decide on a colour palette for your holiday and (with the exception of neutrals and denim) only select items of clothing that fall within that colour palette. Hang everything you'd like to take with you on the rail (or lay it on the bed) so you can see what you've got. Lay out any accessories you think will go with your holiday wardrobe. Pick the hat that comes closest to going with everything, the shoes, handbag and clutch that fit best with your colours.

Once you think you have everything laid out, get tough. Do you really need more than one pair of jeans, a day dress, evening dress and kaftan to pop over swimwear? Pack with an editor's eye, weeding out everything that's not essential, and you'll find you pack a versatile selection of clothes and accessories that you can mix and match.

SAND DUNES
IN ABU DHABI;
SNORKELLING
ON THE GREAT
BARRIER REEF;
AND PARTY TIME
IN SYDNEY

I LOVE GETTING ORGANISED: *MY STYLE*

My holiday essentials

Whether I'm off on holidays or a business trip, certain items always make their way into my suitcase. I never leave home without these travel essentials.

● A SCARF

It can get cold on planes, and the temperature at your destination might be very different from what it was at your departure. Pack a scarf in your handbag and you'll always be comfortable.

● A PARASOL

My big sister taught me that a parasol is a genius way to protect my skin from sunburn and strap marks. She bought me a compact black one and a white one from Tokyo, and I never venture to sunny climes without one. It fits easily in my suitcase for flying and I transfer it into my handbag on arrival.

LOVE A HAT: IT HIDES A MULTITUDE OF FOLLICULAR SINS

• A FLAT BAG

Cheap, cheerful and perfect for the beach, gym or for packing overflow if you've gone overboard in the shopping department. Best of all, it's easy to pack in the bottom of your suitcase.

• A FAN

I first became a fan of the fan in Ibiza, where the nights are hot and the clubs and outdoor restaurant/cafés can get hot, stuffy and airless. They're incredibly handy and rather fabulous for flirting behind as well.

• A HAT (OR TWO)

The perfect solution to aeroplane frizz. Scrape your hair back, pop a hat and sunglasses on, and you can cover up a multitude of follicular sins. A sports cap is another holiday essential so I don't have to style my hair before I go walking or working out.

• SUNGLASSES

So much more than a fashion accessory… Only wear glasses that mention UV protection and block both UVA and UVB rays.

I LOVE GETTING ORGANISED: *MY STYLE*

My packing technique

When I was 19 years old and heading off on my first tour, my friend Lori's mum, Ruth, taught me how to pack. Forget everything you've ever read about rolling your clothes when you pack them – the secret I was taught is to pack things with the fewest creases possible so there's less ironing on arrival and finding things is easier. Follow my friend's mum's packing technique, and I guarantee you, your wardrobe will be ready to wear on arrival.

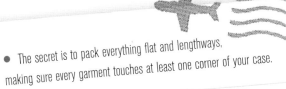

- The secret is to pack everything flat and lengthways, making sure every garment touches at least one corner of your case.

- Pack jeans with the waistband in one corner of your case, with one fold as far down the leg as possible. If you pack one pair of jeans with the heavy (waistband) end in one corner of your case, make sure you pack the next pair with the heavy end in the diagonally opposite corner.

- Do up every second button on your shirts so they hold their shape. Lay them flat in your case so the body is uncreased, then fold the arms in at the shoulder seam so the sleeves are crease-free.

- Lie skirts flat and, if they're maxi, fold them once – ideally on a seam if there is one, or as low down in the skirt as possible.

- Fold long dresses at the waist if they have a seam, otherwise, try to lay as much as possible of the dress flat, folding once at the bottom to minimise ironing.

- Keep layering back and forth, packing from corner to corner, filling every part of the case and keeping everything as flat as possible until all your clothes are in.

- Then pack your shoes, in their shoe bags, in the corners of your case before filling the space in the middle with your toiletry and make-up bags, your swimwear, jewellery boxes and any fragile items.

- Close your case and, as long as it's full, everything should still be in the same place when you arrive at your destination.

- When you re-open your case, take out your shoes and other loose bits, then slide your hand under each corner, lift it gently and look through the layers. Because you've packed everything into at least one corner you can locate clothing without rummaging. Because you've kept folding to a minimum it should be pretty quick to iron out any creases.

What a great way to pack...Thanks Ruth!

CLOSET
PERFECT

I like to group items in the hanging section of my wardrobe: jeans first, followed by tops, shirts, jackets, short dresses, long/evening dresses and finally coats. Then I arrange each section in order from white through the colours of the rainbow, with red first and black last. It makes it so much easier to find clothing quickly! Here are my building blocks of a functional wardrobe:

SHOE RACKS

I like to store the shoes I wear often in shoe racks at the bottom of my wardrobe. The length of the rack is adjustable to fit into the wardrobe and it's stackable, so I can build upwards if I need to.

SHOE BOXES

Muji makes shoe boxes perfect for keeping your shoes out of harm's way, in sizes that fit different shoe heights.

HOOKS

Cheap but brilliantly useful, I put a hook on the inside of my wardrobe doors so I can hang options up and compare them while I'm thinking about what to wear. Attach the hooks at the height at which your longest dress can hang without crumpling on the floor.

{ I like to put a HOOK on the
inside of my wardrobe doors
so I can hang options up and
compare them while I'm thinking
about what to wear. }

{ HATBOXES can be gorgeous additions to the décor of a bedroom or walk-in wardrobe. }

HUGGABLE HANGERS

Soft-grip HUGGABLE HANGERS are the perfect antidote to an over-stuffed wardrobe. They are thin, so they save the space usually taken up by oversized hangers, and the fabric grips even soft, silky fabrics so your delicates don't wind up on the wardrobe floor.

HATBOXES

Keep hats and fascinators in boxes to protect them from dust and light. The bonus with hatboxes is that their designs, vintage or modern, can be a gorgeous addition to the décor of a bedroom or walk-in wardrobe.

BOOT INSERTS

Your boots deserve better than to be left crumpled at the bottom of your wardrobe. Inflatable boot shapers are an inexpensive way to take care of your precious investments.

SHOE TREES

Essential for keeping your shoes in shape, my favourites are black velvet foam shoe trees I found in Harrods and also Kurt Geiger. They are the only ones that are small enough for my shoes!

DOOR MIRRORS

I have mirrors on the insides of two adjacent doors on my wardrobe so that, when both doors are open, they face one another. That way I can angle the doors to see what I'm wearing from every viewpoint. It's my 360-degree check.

Seasonal wardrobe organisation

I often travel from hot to cold seasons and back again, so I never get to pack away my out-of-season clothing. So far the only clothes packing I have done is with my maternity wardrobe – but most of that has been hijacked by pregnant buddies! Try space-saver vacuum-seal bags to keep moths at bay and minimise wardrobe space.

My tips for keeping, giving or throwing away:

SHOW ME A WOMAN who's good at editing down her own wardrobe and I'll show you a woman who's *Devil Wears Prada* heartless! I don't think anyone's really good at this. We form emotional bonds with some clothes and accessories that make it nearly impossible to part with them. It's a little easier if you have a friend who you know loves an item that's passed its use-by date in your wardrobe. Cue magnanimous act of supreme couture generosity and some serious brownie points. Weeding out your wardrobe is not a job to be undertaken solo.

TAKE THE PROFESSIONAL APPROACH. It was at the time of my new bob haircut and, with 12 months' planning needed for work, I had to bite the bullet and pay a professional to come in and sort out my wardrobe. I was in hot sweats for a week before she came because I knew it would be terrifying, and I felt like I was having my heart ripped to shreds as I waved goodbye to piles of beloved items. Tough? Yes. But it was so worthwhile, because I knew I'd been

hanging on to things that didn't suit me any more because I was irrationally attached to them. Ultimately the editing process was great, because I only kept things that looked great and made me feel great. I liken that experience to the feeling you get when you're thinking about going to the gym: 'I don't want to go, I don't want to go…' Then you go, and after you've been you feel amazing.

PHONE A FRIEND. I always think it's easier to get someone to help you with this task, so the best option is to get a friend to help you. It really makes a difference having an objective eye. When you don't have an attachment to the clothes it's easy to tell someone else what to hang on to and what to banish.

IF YOU'RE DOING IT YOURSELF, pull out the things you know look fantastic on you because they make you feel great and people compliment you when you're wearing them. If that's only three pieces in your wardrobe, so be it.

ONCE YOU SEE ALL THE DISCARDED PIECES piled up on the bed you'll realise you don't really use them. (A great indicator is whether or not you can be bothered to hang them up again!)

DONATE CLOTHES TO YOUR LOCAL CHARITY SHOP, make a day of selling them at your local market, swap them at a swap-meet or sell them from home through eBay.

IF YOU ALREADY HAVE ENOUGH DUSTERS TO LAST A LIFETIME, there are textile recycling schemes where you can send discarded clothes that are not fit for charity shops. I like Rag Bag (ragbag.co.uk) a nationwide fundraising scheme that pays for every kilogram of textiles collected for recycling and reducing the amount going to landfill.

DONATING CLOTHES:

When donating clothes make sure they are good-quality, clean and wearable. Don't offload badly damaged items to your local charity shop.

LOVING
Who
YOU ARE

Face, body and well-being

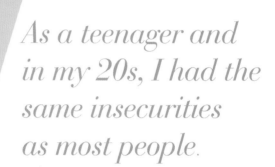

As a teenager and in my 20s, I had the same insecurities as most people.

I particularly struggled with my skin and, because I was on stage performing, it made me feel very self-conscious. It wasn't until I hit my 30s that I really started embracing the things that make me unique. I've spoken to many people who agree that in your 20s you're very up and down – trying to work things out – and that it's not until your 30s that you start to feel comfortable and content with who you are. Over the years I've learned that self-acceptance is the first step to style. Having confidence in that acceptance is the key to making the most of you.

FACE

Everybody's skincare routine is different – the trick is finding what suits you. My friend Tabs isn't massively into wearing make-up and lots of beauty products, but she's absolutely pedantic about moisturising day and night. I'm more obsessed about cleansing and cleaning my skin because I have to wear so much make-up at work. I like nothing more than slapping on a face pack and slipping into a hot bath.

My desert island must-haves

LIP BALM

I'm constantly battling against dry lips so I've tried all sorts of lip balms. Lanolips is one I use a lot, it's cruelty-free, 100% natural and nourishing. It's great if you can find natural products that work. Simon Cowell's make-up artist recommended Shizen Lip Hydrating Serum, and I love it. You just put a few drops on your lips and let it soak in. It smells lovely and is also good for dry cuticles. Tabs swears by her By Terry Rose Balm. She loves anything that contains rose on her skin because it's so gentle and refreshing.

SUN PROTECTION

A little bit of sun on the skin is good for you, helping to boost vitamin D, but I try to stick to times when the sun is at its most gentle and cover up with hats, sunglasses, a big parasol and clothing in intense midday heat. Getting sunburned is really ageing so it's only sensible to cover up.

I LOVE THE
COLOUR OF
MODELCO
TAN MOUSSE

{ There's no denying a GLOW can help lift your mood.

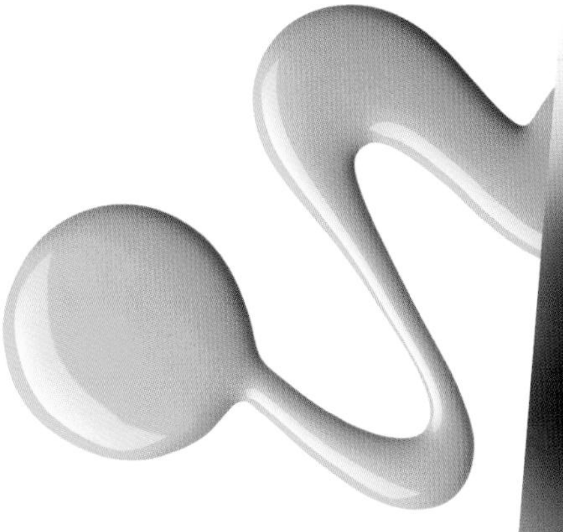

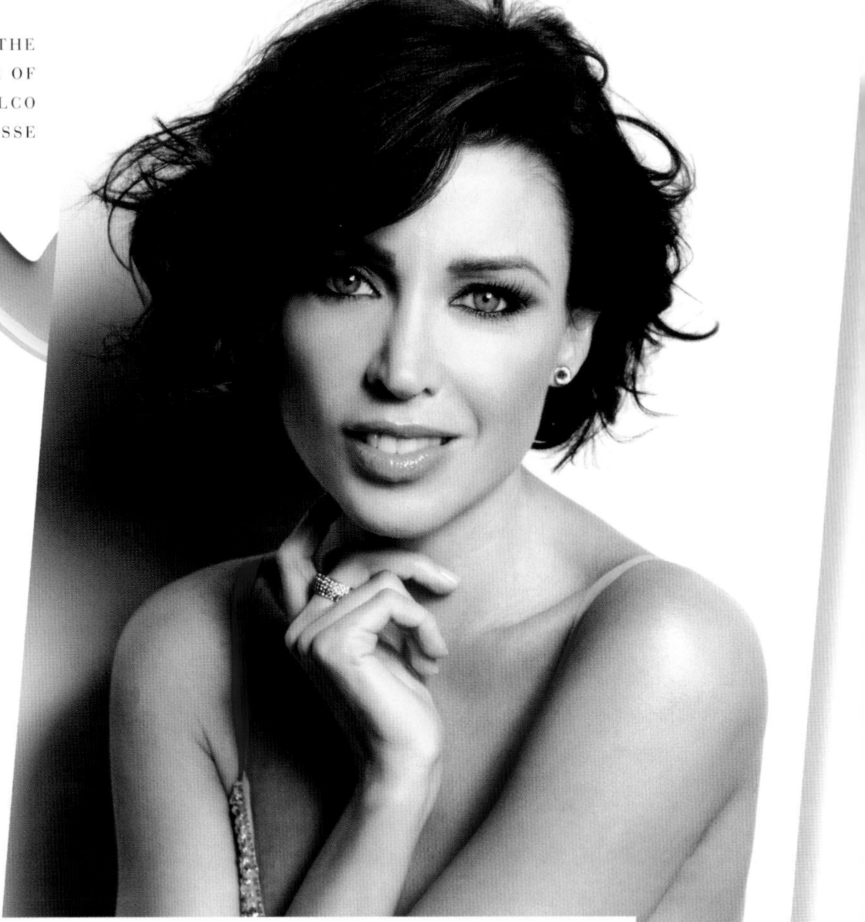

FAKE TAN

It's critical to protect your skin, but there's no denying a glow can help lift your mood, especially in the transition from winter to spring. Mentally it gives me a pick-up and makes me feel better if I'm not staring at my pale, pasty face in a mirror. My UK hair and make-up artist Christian says Jemma Kidd Show Stopper Year Round Body Glow is the 'best glowing skin product ever, in the whole world' for bronzed glossy pins, so it must be good! Tan towels are a mess-free, fuss-free way to apply fake tan and, if you're travelling, they're individually wrapped, keeping your luggage light and removing the risk of tan-soaked clothing from leaky or broken bottles. ModelCo Tan Mousse is a yummy colour that really makes you look like you've been on holiday.

EYE MAKE-UP

The day can't begin until I've done my eye make-up so, if I was in a shipwreck, I'd definitely save an eyebrow pencil, eyelash curler and my amazing ModelCo Fibre Lash mascara (left). The rest could go into the water, but I can't do without those. I like a thick, angled brow shape – Sophia Loren and Audrey Hepburn are my eyebrow icons. I use my eyebrows when I express myself. All the Minogues do, and it's only a matter of time before Ethan learns too.

I USE MY EYEBROWS WHEN I EXPRESS MYSELF. ALL THE MINOGUES DO!

THE EYES HAVE IT: I WOULDN'T BE WITHOUT EYE MAKE-UP

{ When I want to go GLOSSY
and UNDERSTATED, ModelCo
Pink Sea Shell Gloss is gorgeous! }

LIPSTICK

Bright-coloured lips can really give your face and mood a lift, make your teeth look whiter and brighten your eyes. If you feel like adding a splash of colour to your day without planning an entire outfit around it, just get out your lippy! I have a rainbow of lipstick colours. For copper shades I love MAC Matte So Chalo, MAC Sheen Supreme ABO and Illamasqua Scandal. My favourite reds are Illamasqua Box and Ciccone Voluptas. Ciccone Hera is a divine browny-pink shade, and when I want to go glossy and understated, ModelCo Pink Sea Shell Gloss is gorgeous.

NAILS

Like tidy hair, I think nicely manicured nails are a sign of good grooming. I'm very good at painting them myself after years of changing polish to match costumes when I was on tour. If you have a long nail bed like me, you can have your nails quite short and still wear bold colours if you want to. If your nail bed is shorter, you may want to keep your nails longer if you're going to use strong colour. When I want to go pale and girly, Zoya Dannii is a favourite.

GEL NAILS

I still love giving myself a manicure — I find it therapeutic — but I'd rather be playing with Ethan than waiting for my nails to dry for hours. Quick-drying gel is one option, and I like Jessica GELeration and Shellac by Creative Nail Design because they don't damage your natural nails, last well and don't chip or smudge.

Team Dannii

Dannii's hair and make-up maestro Christian Vermaak reveals his must-have products for creating Dannii's flawless locks.

Christian loves:

● Kevin Murphy Session Hair Spray

This spray has serious hold and brushes out nicely without leaving a sticky residue.

● Bumble and Bumble Brown Hair Powder

I like to use this dry shampoo even when hair is clean. It just gives it an added boost to create volume.

● Osis Dust It by Schwarzkopf

It's the best styling dust I have found, and it gives great volume to the hair.

● Head Jog Brushes

I love these hairbrushes as they give the hair a high shine while drying, and the vented barrels help hair to dry more quickly.

ON SET WITH CHRISTIAN VERMAAK, AND CHRISTIAN'S
FAVOURITE STYLE ON THE PIERS MORGAN SHOW (ABOVE RIGHT)

● Cloud Nine The O Heated Rollers

I love these. The pod heats the rollers in four seconds. No more waiting around
for half an hour for rollers to heat!

My favourite style that I've created on Dannii was for her appearance on the
Piers Morgan show. It's a timeless, clean, classic style that will never date. The
thing I love about Dannii's hair is that, no matter what crazy style I create for it,
she defines the style, the style doesn't define her.

{ *MY DEFINITION OF BEAUTY IS A FACE WITH A SMILE. THAT'S WHEN MY BOYFRIEND TELLS ME I LOOK BEAUTIFUL – WHEN I'M LAUGHING AND SMILING.*

Fragrance

Perfume is fun. Like clothing it can change your mood, and I never feel fully dressed until I have my fragrance on.

When we were creating our fragrance, Tabs and I knew roughly what we wanted before we started, which narrowed the search for our signature fragrance considerably. The basis of the scent is a blend of essential oils I love — orange and bergamot — because they are mood enhancers. We added florals and musks to the base notes to give it depth.

ESSENTIAL OILS – My wake-up call

I have a favourite blend of essential oils that I like to burn in the morning to wake myself up: two drops of cinnamon, two drops of peppermint and two drops of orange oil. All my friends associate that blend with me and when I get back from a trip my house doesn't feel like home until I've fired up my diffuser. If I go to a hotel and there's a kettle in the room I'll put boiling water in a mug and pop in the oil drops to fill the room with fragrance. I like to sprinkle a few lavender drops on my pillow before I go to sleep, and I also take a little bottle when I fly and splash a few drops on my seat on the plane to relax me.

WEARING A J'ATON COUTURE DRESS SPECIALLY DESIGNED FOR THE PROJECT D FRAGRANCE CAMPAIGN

BODY

Everyone has their insecurities – it's natural. But there's a level where it's healthy, and a level where it gets out of control and it's unhealthy. If you were born a certain shape and you want to be a different shape, you're being unreasonable with yourself. Embrace your curves or your angles, make the best of what you have and let your personality shine. Class and confidence make any woman look beautiful.

Exercise

Find exercise you LOVE doing and, as well as keeping you fit and trim, it will put a big smile on your face… Like a virtual facelift!

• **LOVELY LEGS** As you can probably tell from photographs over the years, I have never been too keen on showing off my legs. In the past, I found Powerplate and yoga were the best exercises for getting my pins into shape but more recently I've found carrying Ethan around has kept them toned. It must be all the stair-climbing and squatting to pick things up!

• **POUND THE PAVEMENT** Walking doesn't feel like a chore if you're listening to music, pushing a baby in a pram, walking your dog or catching up with a friend. If I make an arrangement to walk with Tabs we chat the entire time, and before we know it we've walked much further than we planned. I tend to take the stairs more when I'm with her too, which is good for the bum and quads. That's what friends are for… I just wish Sergio Rossi and Louboutin made trainers!

POWERPLATE AND YOGA ARE THE BEST EXERCISES FOR KEEPING MY PINS IN SHAPE.

● **SINGING** Did you know that singing exercises the abdominal and facial muscles? When I had singing lessons I learnt to sing from the diaphragm. I always thought I had a naturally flat tummy, then I stopped singing every day and wondered where my little paunch had come from. Now when I'm stuck in the car, or pottering around the house, I turn the radio up and belt out the tunes. (A little air guitar works wonders on the bingo wings too!) Anything that gets your body working really can keep you fit and healthy.

POWERPLATE IN
LONDON AND RUNYON
CANYON HILL CLIMB
IN LOS ANGELES

- **BABY FIT** Running around with Ethan when he was a baby was a bit like weight lifting. Think about it: if you picked up a weight in the gym and held it in one position for ages, eventually your arms would get tired and you'd feel the effects. That's what it is like when you hold your baby. You start chatting to someone and, although it's easy to lose track, you're supporting the baby's weight the entire time. Picking up toys repeatedly (lunging and squatting), lifting the baby out of his stroller, into his high chair and off his change mat (bicep curls), racing up and down the stairs when you forget the wipes, then the nappies (cardio) and you have a full-body workout equal to any local gym class.

- **DO WHAT YOU LOVE, LOVE WHAT YOU DO** Even if you don't feel like exercising, the endorphins always seem to kick in eventually, but I get an extra feel-good kick when I do exercise I love. When I'm on holidays I can go snorkelling for hours and not even realise I'm exercising. If I'm looking forward to exercise I'm hyped up before I even begin, which usually makes for a good workout. Exercise is habitual. I find the more I do it, the more I enjoy doing it.

- **GOOD VIBRATIONS** Before I fell pregnant with Ethan I was a big fan of Powerplate. I used to have 25-minute sessions with an instructor twice a week and found it toned, firmed and reshaped my body fast. It's a perfect exercise option for anyone who's time-poor.

- **GYM CLASS HEROES** I'm a big fan of a class called Body Balance by Les Mills. It's a structured programme that blends yoga, Pilates and t'ai chi. An instructor demonstrates the exercises to music and the class follows along – the music boosts my endorphins and puts me in the mood to exercise. Tabs thinks Body Balance is hilarious. She says I show off, but I've been flexing and stretching in dance classes since I was a kid – it's not my fault I'm flexible! She ends up getting the giggles, then I start laughing and the instructor ends up separating us.

LEARN TO LOVE THE WAY YOU ARE, AND MAKE THE MOST OF YOUR NATURAL ASSETS.

Some tips that help me focus...

● SWEET MUSIC

I think all exercise is easier with music, so I always have my iPod with me when I head out for a workout. My favourite tunes distract me, take my mind off feeling out of breath, and boost my energy levels.

● BE REALISTIC

With work and babies in the mix, there will be some times in your life when it's just not practical to exercise on a daily, or even weekly basis. Be realistic and embrace those times rather than putting pressure on yourself to be a wonder woman.

Having your photo taken

I met J Alexander (far right) at the opening party for the 2009 Melbourne Fashion Festival. He's funny, handsome and incredibly knowledgeable about fashion. He's taught supermodels to walk the runway and has been a judge on *America's Next Top Model* for years, so I wasn't about to waste the opportunity to get some tips on posing for photographs.

Here's what he taught me:

1. Pull up tall as if you have a string attached to the top of your head.

2. Elongate your neck, stretching your head up from your shoulders.

3. Pull the rest of your body in and up.

4. Bevel or 'pop' one knee forward so you twist forward and in, giving you a nice line from the hip through to the ankle.

5. Elongate your bevelled leg by lifting your foot slightly.

Next time I see 'Miss J' I'm hoping he'll give me a lesson on walking the runway so I can get my 'next top model' strut going.

{ When all else fails, just SMILE. I'd rather see a hunchback with their head sunk into their shoulders and a smile than the Hunchback of Notre Dame wearing a scowl or a smirk and trying to look fierce in a picture! }

Miss J Alexander

Confidence equals beauty

Confidence affects everything – the way you feel, the way you appear and the way you interact with people. Notice the things about you that make you feel confident, the things that make you feel the way you want to feel – more assertive, more approachable, more sexy – and rock out your strengths.

Pop star Prince is a great example: he's not a tall, muscle-bound guy, but everyone finds him sexy because of his confidence. He oozes masculinity. Think of Beyoncé's on-stage alter ego Sasha Fierce, whom she invented to help her overcome shyness. If you have to, trick yourself into feeling confident by creating your own super-confident persona. Do it long enough and you'll come to believe it, just like Beyoncé who says she doesn't need Sasha Fierce any more because, 'I've grown and now I'm able to merge the two'.

I know I feel more confident when I'm wearing heels. Whether it's getting fit that makes you feel good, wearing certain clothes, good grooming, focusing on your best attributes or distracting yourself from feeling nervous by concentrating on something else, find what gives you a confidence boost and do it.

PHOTOGRAPHED BY ELISABETH HOFF IN 2007

HAVE A WORD WITH YOURSELF

I've read that if you want to feel confident about something, one of the healthiest things to do is to start a sentence with 'I am' when you are talking about it. Popping sticky notes with affirmations on your bathroom mirror, fridge or workspace is another good tip. Jot your dreams and goals on them and phrase it as if you have already achieved them: 'I am a smart, sassy, successful business woman.' 'I am fabulous rocking out my new stilettos…' You get the idea.

{ *YOU JUST NEED TO ACCEPT AND LOVE WHO YOU ARE, EXACTLY THE WAY YOU ARE.*

FIND YOUR STYLE SPIRIT

Look at the people you admire – your style icons – and ask yourself what it is that draws you to them. Tabs and I both love Jennifer Aniston and Kate Hudson, and we're always saying how much we'd love to see them wearing PROJECT D. They're quite different physically, but they share a similar beachy, relaxed, laid-back essence and I think that's what draws us to them.

If you simply try to wear the same clothes or make-up as your icons it's going to be a lot of hard work – certainly not effortless. Instead, think about the things that make you feel carefree and effortless. Once you work that out and integrate it with your own personal style you'll nail it.

ROCK OUT YOUR DIFFERENCES

When you look at supermodels over the years, it's often the girls who have something different about them who make it big. Cindy Crawford was told she'd never model because of the mole on her lip, but in the end that became her signature. Twiggy was told she wasn't model material because she was petite and skinny; German model Nadja Auermann was 5'11" tall and told she had pole vaulter's legs, and Naomi Campbell had to fight discrimination to get on to the cover of *Vogue* magazine. By celebrating their differences they allowed themselves to be the best they could be, and there's no reason why you can't do that too. You just need to accept and love who you are, exactly the way you are.

'They are my inspiration girls!'

LOVE IT

KATE HUDSON,
JENNIFER
ANISTON, AND
SHARING A HUG
WITH TWIGGY

Love yourself

Some of my most treasured time on the set of Marks & Spencer adverts is when I chat to Twiggy (Lawson) between takes. When you think of the 1960s, you think of her – her androgynous figure perfectly showcased the mood, the make-up and clothes of that era. It's amazing to think what she achieved when you consider she was teased at school for being skinny and having no curves.

As a teenager, people told her she had 'something' and should try modelling, but she saw an agent who told her she was the wrong height and shape to be successful. Twiggy sort of agreed, but she persevered, went to a photoshoot where the photographer just captured her essence, and that was it. She became Britain's first internationally famous teenage model – the face of an era. Twiggy says she was having dinner sometime after that shoot, and the same agent came up to her and said: 'Boy, was I wrong about you.' Twiggy said she wasn't wrong, at the time there just weren't any models of her shape, height or size. It was unheard of. She just made the most of what she had, and in the end she changed perceptions.

So many models on the Marks & Spencer set with us were also teased about being skinny when they were young. They say the thing that got them through was their mum sitting them down and telling them to follow her example and make the best of their shapes.

ON SET WITH FELLOW MARKS & SPENCER GIRLS LISA SNOWDON AND VV BROWN

Where to find...

A

ALANNAH HILL
www.alannahhill.com.au
ALEXANDER MCQUEEN
www.alexandermcqueen.com
AMY JEAN
www.amyjean.com.au
ANNINA VOGEL
www.anninavogel.co.uk
ANNOUSHKA
www.annoushka-jewellery.com
ANYA HINDMARCH
www.anyahindmarch.com
ASTLEY CLARKE
www.astleyclarke.com
ATELIER MAYER
www.atelier-mayer.com

B

BALENCIAGA
www.balenciaga.com
BENJIBOX
www.benjibox.com.au
BENTLEY & SKINNER
www.bentley-skinner.co.uk
BODYMETRICS
www.bodymetrics.com
BRAVADO BRAS
www.bravadodesigns.com
BRUCE OLDFIELD
www.bruceoldfield.com
BY TERRY
www.byterry.com

C

C&C CALIFORNIA
www.candccalifornia.com
CAPEZIO
www.capeziodance.com
CELINE
www.celine.com
CHANEL
www.chanel.com

CHARLOTTE OLYMPIA
www.charlotteolympia.com
CHRISTIAN LACROIX
www.christian-lacroix.fr
CHRISTIAN LOUBOUTIN
www.christianlouboutin.com
CICCONE
www.cicconecosmetics.com
CUTLER AND GROSS
www.cutlerandgross.com

D

DOLCE&GABBANA
www.dolcegabbana.com
DYRBERG/KERN
www.dyrbergkern.com

E

EGG MATERNITY
www.eggmaternity.co.nz
ELIE SAAB
www.eliesaab.com
ELLE MACPHERSON
www.ellemacphersonintimates.com
EMILIA WICKSTEAD
www.emiliawickstead.com

F

FENDI
www.fendi.com

G

GEORGINA GOODMAN
www.georginagoodman.com
GIUSEPPE ZANOTTI
www.giuseppezanottidesign.com
GUCCI
www.gucci.com

H

HARVEY NICHOLS
www.harveynichols.com

HOLLYWOOD FASHION TAPE
www.hollywoodfashionsecrets.com
HOLSTER
www.holsterfashion.com
HOT MILK
www.hotmilklingerie.com

I

ILLAMASQUA
www.illamasqua.com

J

JAMES PERSE
www.jamesperse.com
JASPER CONRAN
www.jasperconran.com
J'ATON
www.jatoncouture.com
J BRAND
www.jbrandjeans.com
J. CREW
www.jcrew.com
JENNY PACKHAM
www.jennypackham.com
JESSICA
www.jessicacosmetics.co.uk
JOOAL
www.jooalinternational.com
JULIEN MACDONALD
www.julienmacdonald.com

K

KRMA
www.krmaclothing.com

L

LANOLIPS
www.lanolips.com
LANVIN
www.lanvin.com
LARIZIA
www.larizia.com

LEVI'S
www.eu.levi.com
www.levis.com.au
LINDSAY PHILLIPS
www.lindsay-phillips.co.uk
LISA HO
www.lisaho.com
LOLA ROSE
www.lolarose.co.uk
LOUIS VUITTON
www.louisvuitton.com
LULU GUINNESS
www.luluguinness.com

M
MAC
www.maccosmetics.co.uk
www.maccosmetics.com.au
MAKE UP STORE
www.makeupstore.se
MALENE BIRGER
www.bymalenebirger.com
MAMAS AND PAPAS
www.mamasandpapas.com
MANOLO BLAHNIK
www.manoloblahnik.com
MARCHESA
www.marchesa.com
MARKS & SPENCER
www.marksandspencer.com
MARTIN GRANT PARIS
www.martingrantparis.com
MELISSA ODABASH
www.odabash.com
METALICUS
www.metalicus.com
MICHAEL KORS
www.michaelkors.com
MODELCO
www.modelco.com.au
MOTHERCARE
www.mothercare.com
MUJI
www.mujionline.co.uk
MYLA
www.myla.com
MY SWEET BELLY COUTURE
www.sweet-belly.de

MY-WARDROBE.COM
www.my-wardrobe.com

N
NARS
www.narscosmetics.co.uk
NET-A-PORTER
www.net-a-porter.com
NICHOLAS KIRKWOOD
www.nicholaskirkwood.com

O
OLIVER BONAS
www.oliverbonas.com
OZITUDE
www.ozitude.com

P
PAIGE MATERNITY
www.paigeusa.com
PAULE KA
www.pauleka.com
PHILIP TREACY
www.philiptreacy.co.uk
PINK LOULOU
www.pinkloulou.com
PLEASURE STATE
www.pleasurestate.com
POMELLATO
www.pomellato.it
PROJECT D
www.projectdonline.co.uk

R
RALPH & RUSSO
www.ralphandrusso.com
RETROSUN
www.retrosun.co.uk
RIPE MATERNITY
www.ripematernity.com
ROLAND MOURET
www.rolandmouret.com
RUBY & GINGER
www.rubyandginger.co.uk

S
SAMSONITE
www.samsonite.com

SELFRIDGES
www.selfridges.com
SERAPHINE
www.seraphine.com
SERGIO ROSSI
www.sergiorossi.com
SHIZEN
www.shizen.com.au
SLACKS & CO
www.slacksandco.com
SOLANGE AZUGARY
PARTRIDGE
www.solangeazugary
partridge.com
SPANX
www.spanx.com
SPORTSGIRL
www.sportsgirl.com.au
STEPHANIE SCHELL
www.stephanieschell.com
STEPHEN WEBSTER
www.stephenwebster.com

T
TABITHA
www.tabitha.uk.com
TALISMAN GALLERY
www.talismangallery.co.uk
TOPSHOP
www.topshop.com

V
VALENTINO
www.valentino.com
VICTORIA BECKHAM
www.victoriabeckham.com

Y
YEOJIN BAE
www.yeojinbae.com
YVES SAINT LAURENT
www.ysl.com

Z
ZARA
www.zara.com
ZOYA
www.zoya.com

Pictures...

Photography © Jonty Davies, except for the following:

© Alamy: 127. © Georges Antoni: 145, 165. Author collection © KDB Artists Pty Ltd: 6, 14, 15, 16 (left),19 (left), 20, 21 (top right & bottom right), 22, 23, 24 (top), 25, 30 (right), 73 (left), 79, 39 (right), 157 (left), 162 (middle & left), 200, 212, 241, 245 (right), 249 (bottom). © BIGPICTURESPHOTO. COM: 55/photo Greg Sirc & David Boyes, 124. © Lee Broomfield: 13, 123. © Channel Seven: 21 (top left). © Chris Colls: 141, 239, 255. © Corbis: 40 (right) & 41 (top left)/photos Hulton-Deutsch Collection, 41 (bottom & top right), 44 (bottom) & 46 (left)/photos Bettmann, 45/photo Sunset Boulevard, 46 (right)/photo John Springer Collection, 52/photo Conde Nast Archive. © Chris Craymer: 193. © Robert Fairer: 148, 149, 159, 160, 161. © Daniela Federici: 48 (right). © Fremantle Media Enterprises (FME): 92 (top), 93 (left & right). © Getty Images: 5/photo Dave Hogan, 28 (bottom)/photo Tony Barson, 28 (top)/photo Dave Benett, 31 (top) & 70 (right)/photos Ferdaus Shamim, 38/photo Time & Life Pictures, 40 (left) & 195 (left & middle)/photos Roger Viollet, 69 (left)/photo Lucas Dawson, 43 (top) & 47 & 49/photos Moviepix, 53 (right)/photo Popperfoto, 55 (left), 55 (top middle)/photo Eamonn McCormack, 55 (top right)/photo Film Magic, 56 (top), 56 (bottom)/photo Larry Busacca, 57, 66 & 72 (top) & 129 (right)/photos Ian Gavan, 68 (left) & 70 (left) & 139 (left)/photos Mike Marsland, 68 (right)/photo Samir Hussein, 69 (right)/photo Cameron Spencer, 71/photo Dani Abramowicz, 72 (bottom), 73 (right)/photo Serge Thomann, 100/photo Ernst Haas, 103/photo Frank Worth, 121 (right)/ photo Neil Mockford, 125 (right)/photo Graham Denholm, 157 (right)/photo Don Arnold, 167/photo Lisa Maree Williams, 179 (bottom)/photo Tom Schierlitz, 249 (left)/photo Mark Mainz, 249 (top right). © Chris Gloag: 82, 186, 187 (left), 190, 191, 199, 201, 209, 217 (left), 218, 219, 230, 231. © René Gruau Sarl www.renegruau.com: 39 (left). © David Gubert: 131, 132, 135, 205. © Elisabeth Hoff: 147, 238 (left), 247, 256. © Nicky Johnston/Heat Magazine: 243. Courtesy KDB Artists Pty Ltd: 7, 29, 211 (bottom left & right). © Marks & Spencer: 251/photo Uli Weber. © Mattel Inc: 54 (top left & bottom). Sean McMenomy © KDB Artists Pty Ltd: 189. © Photoshot: 44 (top)/photo LFI, 121 (top)/photo Retna Pictures. © The Picture Library Ltd: 67/photo Alan Davidson. © Press Association Images: 39 (right), 42 (left)/photo Topham, 42 (right), 54 (top left)/photo Othoniel Patrick. Courtesy Project D: 129 (left), 153/ photo David Brook, 238 (right). © Rex Features: 125 (left)/photos David Fisher, 43 (bottom), 48 (left)/ photo Everett Collection, 53 (left)/photo Daily Mail, 121 (bottom)/photo Media Mode, 151/photo Fiona Hamilton, 163, 235 (top right)/photo ITV. © Robin Sellick: 195 (right). Ken Sharp © KDB Artists Pty Ltd: 24 (bottom). Nathan Smith © KDB Artists Pty Ltd: 92 (bottom), 93 (middle), 179 (top left & top right), 210, 211 (top), 235 (top left & bottom left). © Splash News: 213/photo Martin Grimes. © Simon Upton: 229. © Christian Vermaak: 104, 184, 185, 234, 235 (middle & bottom right). © XPOSUREPHOTOS. COM: 162 (right). © Johnny Young/YTT: 16 (right), 17, 19 (right).

Thanks to Annoushka, Dolce&Gabbana, Harvey Nichols, J'Aton, Larizia , Ralph & Russo, Stephen Webster and many others for the loan of clothes, shoes and jewellery for the book; and to Milton Hammon for all his *Young Talent Time* assistance.

With thanks...

We all have to start somewhere... for me it was neon socks, big hair and shoulder pads! Thanks to my grandma, Millie, who taught me to sew, and to all the many photographers, stylists, hair and make-up artists and amazing fashion designers over the years who have helped me find My Style. Thank you to these wonderful people who helped make my dream book possible:

Melissa Le Gear, Mark Klemens and Nathan Smith at Profile Talent Management

Pat Lomax at Bell Lomax Moreton Agency

Ami Richards, Francine Lawrence, Emma Harrow, Kerr MacRae and everyone at Simon & Schuster

Charlotte James, who brought my words to life

Nikki Dupin and Jane de Teliga

Jonty Davies and the photographic team

Angie Smith

Christian Vermaak

Fotini Hatzis

Simon Jones and Alex Mullen from Hackford Jones PR

Tabitha Somerset Webb – Project D

Kylie Minogue

Twiggy

Miss J Alexander

My beauty and nutrition advisor, Dr Ranj

Jacob and Anthony from J'Aton Couture

Tamara and Michael from Ralph & Russo

Dorothy and the girls at Dorothy Couture

Thanks to Nate for the DJ set of retro heaven 'choons'

Special thanks to Bonnie Kirkman and Harriet Lomax who keep Team Minogue running...always!

FINALLY...eternal love and thanks to Kris and my family Ron, Carol, Kylie and Brendan

PS You are never too old for a dress-up box.

PPS A special mention for Ethan, who has filled my world with so much joy and keeps me on my toes. Mummy now feels just as happy in flats as she does in heels!